"Explores the redemptive, restorativ[...]
plants, and flowers. . . . Her 'inner g[...]
process that both feeds and is fed b[...]
gracefully detailed here."

Body Mind Spirit

"How gardening can clean the layers of soot and grime off your
intuition, can help you listen better to that intuition and act on it.
Consider Handelsman the facilitator of a seminar that will force
you to slow down, grow up, fine-tune and take responsibility."

—*Los Angeles Times*

"Articulate, wise, entertaining, but most of all, real and believable . . .
a must read."   —Louise Collins, *The Louise Collins Show*

"True perception . . . and unusual insights are mixed in . . . this
collection of linked essays about coming of age as a gardener and as
a woman."   —*Kirkus Reviews*

"The deep levels of love and connection with plants—the healing
power of 'inner gardening' . . . assure gardeners that the dividends
are ample for both them and their flowers."   —*Booklist*

"I was embraced by it. It was a delight to read."
          —Dorothy Maclean, cofounder of Findhorn

"Inspired by *Growing Myself*, I conducted a small experiment. One of
the chores I've always hated most is repotting. Handelsman's
advice: Give a day's notice. So I had a talk with my peace lily. The
next day my peace lily slid right out of the old pot and didn't wilt.
Coincidence? I don't think so."   —Cheryl Merser, *New Woman*

"Full of amazing tales about what is possible if we give plants the
respect they deserve. Hot tips for becoming an 'inner gardener'
yourself."   —*Yoga Journal*

JUDITH HANDELSMAN has been gardening columnist for *Vogue* and
New Age Journal. She coauthored *Greenworks: Tender Loving Care for
Plants*. Her last book, *Gardens from Garbage: How to Grow Indoor Plants
from Recycled Kitchen Scraps*, was cited as one of the best children's
books of 1993. She regularly lectures and conducts workshops, and
lives in Laguna Beach, California.

growing myself

a spiritual journey through gardening

Judith Handelsman

A PLUME BOOK

PLUME
Published by the Penguin Group
Penguin Books USA Inc., 375 Hudson Street,
New York, New York 10014, U.S.A.
Penguin Books Ltd, 27 Wrights Lane, London W8 5TZ, England
Penguin Books Australia Ltd, Ringwood, Victoria, Australia
Penguin Books Canada Ltd, 10 Alcorn Avenue,
Toronto, Ontario, Canada M4V 3B2
Penguin Books (N.Z.) Ltd, 182–190 Wairau Road,
Auckland 10, New Zealand

Penguin Books Ltd, Registered Offices:
Harmondsworth, Middlesex, England

Published by Plume, an imprint of Dutton Signet,
a division of Penguin Books USA Inc.
Previously published in a Dutton edition.

First Plume Printing, June, 1997
2 4 6 8 10 9 7 5 3 1

Ⓟ REGISTERED TRADEMARK—MARCA REGISTRADA

The Library of Congress has catalogued the Dutton edition as follows:
Handelsman, Judith F.
Growing myself : a spiritual journey through gardening /
Judith Handelsman.
p.   cm.
Includes bibliographical references.
ISBN 0-525-94057-X (hc.)
ISBN 0-452-27517-2 (pbk.)
1. Handelsman, Judith F.   2. Horticultural writers—United States—
Biography.   I. Title.
SB63.H35A3   1996
635'.01—dc20   96-308
                                             CIP

Printed in the United States of America
Original hardcover design by Eve L. Kirch

For my mother, Nina, who has always stood by me. This book could not have been born without her help.

And thanks to *Joan Blue*, for her ceaseless love and unwavering belief in me; *Gloria Kamler*, for the richness and longevity of our friendship; and *Barbara Horton*, for the integrity of our work together.

He who cultivates a garden, and brings to perfection flowers and fruits, cultivates and advances at the same time his own nature.

—Ezra Weston,
Massachusetts Horticultural Society, 1845

The temple bell stops
But I still hear the sound
coming out of the flowers.

—Basho, Japanese Zen poet (1644–94)

Never forget:
we walk on hell
gazing at flowers.

—Issa, Japanese Zen poet (1763–1827)

Contents

Author's Note

Simone Weil, the twentieth-century theologian, once said the only real question to be asked of another is "What are you going through?" It struck me when I read those words that here was another person fascinated with my favorite fundamental question: how does one manage with what one has been dealt?

My ability to manage in the world gradually ripened through my love of plants. Gardening became my absorbing passion, plants my teachers and best friends. Taking care of plants soothed me when life was difficult and invigorated me on an average or good day.

One of my life's struggles has been to discover my calling, to find a purpose in whatever I did. Gradually it dawned on me that I could write and speak publicly about what mattered to me most. I could tell the truth about what I learned about myself and my life through gardening.

When I first started writing down my love story with

plants, I was simply writing what I knew, what was important to me. Then, as I reached out in talks and in the media, I began to realize that there were other people who felt deep levels of love and connection when they gardened or allowed themselves to just "be" with the natural world. These people practiced what I call inner gardening: they had relationships with trees and other plants.

Some of them felt silly admitting the existence of this relationship. Husbands laughed at them or wives told them that they were crazy. They didn't dare mention such a thing at gardening-club meetings or to neighbors over the back fence. These people learned to keep their mouths shut and their feelings a secret—except from their fellow inner gardeners. *Growing Myself* is my offering to help those trapped in this closet to come out. And to others who have never considered the possibility of approaching gardening through a relationship with plants, I hope to awaken you to a way of being in the world that brings enormous happiness and great beauty.

Judith Handelsman
Laguna Beach, California
1995

ONE

Preparing the Soil

If you wish to make anything grow, you must understand it, and understand it in a very real sense. "Green Fingers" are a fact, and a mystery only to the unpracticed. But green fingers are an extension of a verdant heart.

—Russell Page, *The Education of a Gardener*

You might say the seeds of this book germinated in Brazil when, at twenty-three, I accompanied my mother to Rio de Janeiro after the death there of my aunt Patsy, my mother's younger sister. Our families were very close, and I had a special affinity for Patsy because she was a spiritual seeker. Her daughter, Mossa, was a good friend of mine and the only other person who ever spoke to me of spiritual matters.

Patsy wanted to be cremated. She asked to have her ashes scattered in the ocean bordering the city she had lived in and loved for the last fifteen years of her life.

Mossa had the daunting task of going up in an open helicopter and doing the job nobody else wanted to do. Out of a mixture of guilt and courage, I said yes when she asked me to go with her.

Once up in the air, we opened the large mahogany box of Patsy's cremated remains, and, instead of dust as we had expected, we were surprised by what looked like large clumps of sun-baked coral. We scooped out handfuls of this unpulverized bone and threw it out to the wind, yelling over the noise of the engine for Patsy to have a good journey.

The experience left me shaken. For months after I returned to New York, my heart felt raw and life seemed tasteless and meaningless. Patsy was the first person I had been close to who died. Her departure left a void that was almost tangible. Confronting the death and loss of a loved one for the first time in my life made me ask questions I had never asked before. Why was I here? What was the purpose of life? And what did it all mean, anyway?

During this time, I met my future husband, a journalist who was asking himself the same sort of questions. Since we both seemed to be on a similar course, we returned to Brazil to find our answers. Brazil was supposed to be the first leg of a spiritual journey around the world. We were on a spiritual quest and we wanted to find *it*, whatever *it* was. *It* was a big nebulous *it*; a magical Something that would enlighten us and allow us to do everything right. Life's problems wouldn't exist for us. This is an overstatement, of course, but it might give you some idea of how unenlightened my idea of enlightenment was.

We settled for a few months in a tiny mountain town called Novo Friburgo, just three hours outside of Rio, where we rented a house on top of Hungarian Hill, a place filled with Swiss, Germans, and, of course, Hungarians. Alpine plants, flowers, and trees blended in with the tropical vegetation, so the expatriates felt right at home. There were pine trees and red papaya, icy white azaleas and mangoes galore.

In the mornings, we practiced yoga at a nearby hotel retreat called Templo de Yoga. People came there from the cities for rest and relaxation. The teachers held classes in a rosewood room lined with shoji screens that slid open onto a rushing creek. The sound of the water made that room seem eternal. It could have been anywhere in the world—China, Japan, even Tibet.

Every morning the altar was freshly decorated. It consisted of a large, round, flat handmade basket painted with a black-and-white yin/yang symbol of the Tao in the center. On either side of this simple icon sat a flower vase. One contained exquisitely vital dew-covered white roses; the other, equally fresh and fragrant red roses. I learned more from that room and how it was loved than from any words the teachers ever spoke.

After class, we would walk home to our house atop Hungarian Hill, zigzagging up a steep mountainside switchback through wilderness. In order to reach the ascending path, we had to walk on a flat stretch of dirt road bordered on both sides with dense vegetation. One day as we walked in the hot noonday sun, I looked down the dusty road, and stretched out in front of me were thousands and thousands of butterflies emerging from their co-coons.

That moment was like walking into a birthing room filled with millions of babies being born. I just stood there transfixed, watching a metamorphosis I had only read about in *National Geographic*. When I got home, I lay down on my cot and closed my eyes. Then, for the first time in my life, I had a spiritual experience like one they wrote about in the *New York Times* magazine section. In an article I had read before we left the country, the reporter referred to a survey concerning the spirituality of the American public. One of the questions was "Have you ever had a spiritual experience?" Apparently, seventy-five percent of the American people polled said they had. I thought at the time, in 1973, that that was quite a hefty number. I remember wondering then what defined a spiritual experience. But I figured it was like an orgasm. If you had one, you knew.

So there I was in Brazil, lying down on my cot resting, with my eyes closed and boom! There it was. A voice. Not in the room but inside me. One I could hear but not with my ears. It sounded like my Aunt Patsy's voice. The voice said, "It's not the outer life that matters. It's your inner life that really counts."

I waited for more. I wanted more. But nothing came. I opened my eyes and looked around the room. It was quiet. I was alone.

Whoa, I thought. What was that? Did I imagine it? No. I sensed the truth of the words I'd heard; something real had occurred. A door had opened. From that moment on, I was on a path. In retrospect, I had two awakenings in Brazil. One was hearing the spiritual voice; the other one was an awakening to the voices of the natural world, the realm of trees, plants, and flowers.

Having been born and raised in Manhattan, I knew little of nature except Central Park and the zoo. I have a fleeting but vivid memory of my manic-depressive grandfather, Buck, a gardener, who suffered through electroshock treatments, the therapy in those days for depression. I never heard Grandpa utter a full sentence, but when he worked in his garden, he was a peaceful, happy man. His face, which normally looked tense and frightened, relaxed; his manner lightened, and his eyes came back to life. Grandpa Buck tended a wildly prolific garden on two acres of land across the road from his house in Mount Kisco, New York. Occasionally, my mother and I went up for weekends.

A hedge of blue hydrangeas surrounded the house like a moat. Massive shade-giving elm trees cooled us everywhere on the grounds. Down the hillside slope, a garden teemed with beefsteak tomatoes, white cabbages, sweet baby carrots, and pickling cucumbers that covered the wooden fence defining the border.

Grandpa cut large heads of Bibb lettuce for our meals and filled earthenware jugs on the porch outside the kitchen door with pickles and sauerkraut. On hot summer days it was lovely to dip my fingers into the cool barrels and pluck a few kosher dills to eat. Those days in the garden and evenings on the screened-in porch were rare, special moments. We never stayed in the country for very long.

At sixteen, I went to the University of Wisconsin at Madison. My formative years had been spent in the fast lane of the private-school set in Manhattan, so culture shock registered off the scale that first morning, when, at 7:45, I trudged up Bascom Hill, slipping on the ice, wondering what I was doing there; they closed the schools in New York City when it snowed like that.

My schedule included botany, three hours in the lab every Monday morning to fulfill my science requirement. Having been one of those English and humanities kids, science definitely made me nervous. Put me in a math or science class, and my circuits blew. I steeled myself for the worst and begged the powers that be to make it okay. Surprisingly, botany wasn't so bad.

Drawing the life cycles of plants was my favorite part of the course. I was in awe of the intelligent process plants undergo in order to leaf, flower, fruit, and then die to begin anew. There was poetry and soul to it. I couldn't identify that tender feeling gathering inside me when I studied those life-cycle drawings. All I knew was that I was deeply moved by the serene loveliness of plant life and its simple demonstration of the cyclical process of life and death. Examining the beauty of nature in detail awakened an interest in me I had never had before. Nevertheless, I still succumbed to mental blocks when test time came around. I deserved a D, but the teaching assistant felt sorry for me. I got a C in botany but fell in love with plants.

After that, indoor gardening became my specialty. I discovered a latent talent for making things grow and a gift when it came to nurturing houseplants, I was extremely pleased I had a gift for something. Coleus were my favorites. I loved how they turned their faces toward the light, every leaf staring in the same direction. Every day, I observed, they made a complete about-face, so I rotated them often to help them maintain their balance. It wasn't too hard to figure out. They'd look hunched over and stooped if I didn't.

Caring for houseplants was a way I could nurture and bill and coo and have babies and friends without the tension of having them talk back, except in the kindest fashion . . . silence! With them, I could be myself and not worry about what they thought of me.

After college I moved back to New York. I found a friend who felt the way I did about plants. We both had plant collections we talked about incessantly, and we giggled a lot about how cute each plant personality seemed to be. We enjoyed taking care of them so much we started an indoor-outdoor landscaping business. Landscape design and maintenance for corporations, restaurants, and residences was the service we offered.

The indoor plant craze of the early seventies had barely begun. We became "the plant doctors" and fashioned a niche for ourselves doing what we loved. I had always wanted to write a book, so I combined my passion for plants with my desire to write, and my partner and I produced a layman's guide to growing indoor plants.

It was during this period that my future husband and I traveled to Brazil. When we first arrived, we drove for three days to the north, to Bahia for Carnival. A center of

African influence, Bahia was infamous for being the city where Carnival was wildest.

Can you imagine this? Two intellectuals from Manhattan, having just arrived, pale and tired, from a winter of fighting rush hour on the New York City subway, accustomed to reading about Carnival in the *New York Times*, rushing headlong into the five-day, once-a-year celebration of letting loose in the tropics. We found ourselves a little panicked when the swell of frenzied dancers that followed behind giant floats scooped us up in their path, rendering us helpless as the crowd moved in primitive musical abandon.

It took us months to assimilate into the slow-paced beach-body mentality of the Brazilians. That was when I knew I had been paying too much attention to building my mind and not enough to my physical self. Eventually, we made friends with another couple on Hungarian Hill. The first time we visited their log cabin, perched high above the town, they took us behind the house to visit their vegetable garden. For me it was love at first sight. The perfectly formed lettuce, the firm, upright scallions, and the exotic coriander looked so real they actually seemed artificial. That's how jaded my city eye had become.

Evenly spaced and well-weeded rows orchestrated the luster of the garden. Immediately, I wanted an outdoor garden, and I promised myself I would learn how to grow one. When one of our friends handed me a basket and asked me to pick the vegetables for the evening meal, I became slightly embarrassed. I admitted I had never picked vegetables before. Since I didn't want to hurt anything, I asked her to teach me.

It certainly wasn't very difficult, I marveled, entirely the urban innocent as, starry-eyed and hushed, I followed her through the garden. I kept hearing a little voice inside me saying, *you can do this, you can grow us, too.* I pretended I didn't hear it. In fact, I didn't connect the voice to the actual plants until a couple of years later.

Eventually we traveled throughout Argentina; from Buenos Aires, that old and elegant Paris of South America, down to Patagonia, up to Lake Titicaca in Peru, and finally to Iguaçú Falls, one of the largest waterfalls in the world. There, the borders of three countries meet—Brazil, Paraguay, and Argentina—at a dramatic vortex of electric power.

At this juncture in our trip, Richard Nixon was about to become the first president of the United States to resign from office. We found ourselves drinking coffee and haunting newsstands, spending more time reading the *International Herald Tribune* and *Time* magazine than focusing on our spiritual journey, so we moved back to New York City so as not to "miss anything." To assuage my desire for a vegetable garden, I bought houseplants, as many as I could and still have furniture.

Then, in our own backyard, so to speak, the spiritual answer I was seeking materialized. Teetering high above any connection to the ground, on the sixteenth floor of an apartment house, I made contact with nature. I began communicating with my plants. Not just chitchat as you might imagine, but real talk. I let down my defenses, let go of my preconceived notions of what was real or possible, and simply did what I felt like doing, no matter how crazy it seemed. Through thought, word, and deed I communicated with my plants and they responded. In their own silent way, they communicated back to me. It was clear, as clear as my Aunt Patsy's voice that day on Hungarian Hill—the plants were sentient beings, and I had opened a channel to make their acquaintance. In the beginning, I could hardly believe I was actually conversing with them, but, then again, I used to think people who talked to their animals were weird.

During my early years of experimentation, I had a plant business and worked at home as a writer, so I had a life that allowed for a great deal of gardening time. I spent hours playing with my plants. However, I do want to emphasize that all of one's free time does not necessarily have to be spent with plants in order to reap the benefits of inner gardening. Nor does a person have to be a technical expert to commune with plants. Sometimes it can even get in the way.

As thinking, feeling beings, we have an untapped potential to relate to the plant world. We in the United States at the end of the twentieth century have been raised in deep denial and with great superstition of anything unscientific and nonrational. We have rejected such time-honored aspects of ourselves as imagination, intuition, magic, and self-healing. Until now, we have been missing a lot.

Our consumer culture has advertised the message that materialism brings happiness. Now we are finding out that in the process of accumulating more things, we have no time for ourselves. We are exhausted and disillusioned. There is a big, gaping hole of emptiness, a gnawing feeling that something essential is lacking.

And so, more and more of us are openly exploring the possibility of intangible, unprovable realities that parallel our own carefully observed material world. A growing wave of people within our society is turning inward to find answers and solace.

There is a beautiful quote from the *I Ching* (or *Book of Changes*), the oracle of ancient Chinese wisdom that describes the oneness of both inner and outer realities. "All that is visible must grow beyond itself, extend into the realm of the invisible. Thereby it receives its true consecration and clarity and takes firm root in the cosmic order. . . . The truly divine does not manifest itself apart from man."

This axiom works both ways. The material and nonmaterial worlds are integral parts of each other. They work together. The invisible needs grounding in the concrete, the miracle of life becomes visible in the material world. If we can accept this connection with people and animals, plants are the next logical step as members of a group we acknowledge to be living beings.

In the Native American tradition, notice was given to both plants and animals before harvesting or hunting. The Indians stated their intent, asked permission, and called for volunteers. In an excerpt from her book *Singing for Power: The Song Magic of the Papago Indians of Southern Arizona*, Ruth Underhill describes this common practice:

The Papago . . . stands at the edge of the field. . . . Kneeling, he makes his hole and speaks to the seed, in the Papago manner of explaining all acts to Nature lest there be misunderstanding: "Now I place you in the ground. You will grow tall. Then, they shall eat, my children and my friends. . . ." Night after night, the planter walks around his field "singing up the corn. . . ." Sometimes, all the men of a village meet together and sing all night, not only for the corn but also for the beans, the squash, and the wild things.

I began to develop this attitude step by tentative step, ignorance and innocence proving to be assets. I embarked upon a course of education that would introduce me to the world of inner gardening. I never saw the teacher's face. It took me a while to learn the language. But I grew to love the teacher and the teaching, and, best of all, there were no tests.

TWO

Patience and the Spider Plant

. . . they all participated so deeply of one another's being that the experience could almost be called mystical. For instance, he seemed to know what it actually felt like to be a lizard . . . or starry-eyed amaryllis . . . he was back in the moment which our European fairy-tale books described as the time when birds, beasts, plants, trees, and men shared a common tongue, and the whole world, night and day, resounded like the surf of a coral sea with universal conversation.

—Laurens van der Post, speaking about the
Bushmen in *The Lost World of the Kalahari*

One day, when I was about seven, my mother took me to the basement of our apartment house to do the laundry. The walls and floors were painted military gray, and the low ceiling displayed a complex warp and woof of pipes and tubing. It felt claustrophobic as we navigated our way down and around long corridors until we reached the laundry room.

While she loaded the washing machines, I sat mesmer-
ized watching the soapsuds sloshing around the tiny circular windows. At some point, I stood up and walked out the
back door for some air. When I stepped over the thresh-
old, instead of the usual view of buildings and streets, I saw
a cloud bank of cool light brighter than any sunshine I had
ever seen. Through these clouds I could see another bright
light emanating from its core, friendly but commanding.

Somehow I got the message that this light was the
power behind everything. Although I didn't have words to
describe it, I knew that it meant there was a lot more going
on out there than I had thought. This vision loomed so
large that I automatically tucked it away for future use.

Imbued with this long-forgotten but seminal impression,
I suppose it might have been easier for me, once I started
gardening, to connect in a nontangible way with my plants.
As the years went by, this awareness faded and I seemed to
forget it until my mid-twenties, when my very first incident
as an inner gardener transpired in an apartment house in
New York City, where I lived with my husband.

I had a job writing freelance pieces on all aspects of gardening for NBC All-News Network Radio. The schedule
called for five one-minute spots a week. You may not think
much could be said in one minute, and I myself was surprised to learn how power packed my time could be. My
boss loaned me a stopwatch and directed me to appear in
the studio at the end of each week to voice my gardening
soliloquies. These words of gardening advice were broad-
cast nationwide to the NBC affiliates three times a day.

Once my aunt Gladys heard me on her car radio as she

was crossing the Golden Gate Bridge. This recognition thrilled my mother, and the family was duly impressed. Unfortunately, I was unable to fully enjoy the moment, since I spent a good deal of my time twirling my hair and chewing my lip, trying to crank out my weekly quota of gardening pieces.

One day, a colleague asked me to sit in on an interview with Peter and Eileen Caddy, founders of the Findhorn Community in Scotland. They had just published *The Findhorn Garden* (Harper & Row, 1975) and were doing a publicity tour of America.

The Findhorn Community grew giant vegetables and flowers on the northernmost tip of Scotland in sandy soil and gusty winds, where nothing should have grown. The catch was they were doing it through meditations with the nature spirits and "devas," or angels, of each plant. They were receiving gardening advice directly from such illustrious beings as the sweet pea deva, the lettuce and tomato devas, and Pan himself. I couldn't tell if this was symbolic talk, ideas that existed in their imaginations, or genuine magic. Even with my love for plants it sounded pretty foreign to me.

I couldn't put the book down. It combined magical gardening experiences with practical methodology and described real-life results. I was tickled to discover other people who loved plants the same way I did. Because of the miraculous results, the Findhorn Garden was becoming a pilgrimage mecca for horticultural societies from England, Scotland, and other parts of Europe. I couldn't wait to meet Peter and Eileen Caddy and ask them my most burning spiritual questions. It was still the early days of my spiritual seeking; metaphysics and mystical experience were new concepts to me. I wanted to know more about spiritual growth. When the time came, I asked them both if they thought a person had to suffer in order to grow. They answered simultaneously. She said yes; he said no. We all laughed.

As they left the studio, they invited me to Findhorn. I wanted to go as soon as possible. In the meantime, I went home with new enthusiasm and started to experiment with the ideas proffered by the Findhorn Community.

Houseplants became my subjects. The book said each plant was a being with a soul and an intelligence. I had read of similar ideas from the Druids, the Celts, the ancient Greeks, and the Egyptians. Indigenous cultures around the globe abound with lore about the healing power of plants, not only on the physical level but on the emotional, mental, and spiritual levels as well.

Inspired by the Findhorn example, I started to talk to my houseplants; not just small talk—I related to them as if they were children or beloved pets. Beyond taking care of their physical needs, I began to forge a bond of friendship and love. I gave the plants respect instead of treating them as mere interior decoration.

I decided to use a pot-bound spider plant for my first formal experiment. The plant's tubers were packed in so tightly that I couldn't budge the plant to remove it from its pot. The leaves were starting to lose their nice green color and turn brown and brittle at the tips. There was no soil left, just roots. Since spider plants are tuberous, I knew I could cut this one in half and make two plants out of it.

In the past, the two-step operation of division would inevitably mushroom into an ordeal for me, as well as for the plant. I hated breaking the plastic pots. I'd always cut myself and agonize over sawing the root ball in half, even with a long, suitably sharp kitchen knife. I certainly needed a new system.

The Findhorn Garden suggested giving plants twenty-four-hour notice before doing anything major to them, such as cutting back or transplanting. At this point in my life, communicating with plants was a new concept, and as unusual as the idea sounded at first, it made complete sense to me. I'd certainly want someone to warn me if I was going to have to move, give me notice to prepare myself psychologically as well as logistically.

The Findhorn people said that with twenty-four-hour notice, a plant or shrub could anesthetize itself and do whatever was necessary so it wouldn't go into shock. Leaving part of the procedure up to the plant seemed like a good idea to me. Then the burden of responsibility wasn't wholly on me. The book said that as long as I didn't proceed with a "prove-it-to-me" attitude, giving twenty-four-hour notice would definitely work.

I decided to assume that the spider plant had an intelligence—one beyond my understanding, but an intelligence nonetheless. With this attitude, I left the possibilities wide open. Anything could happen. And why not? It was just as easy to think this way as the other way, that plants just sat there and didn't think or feel anything.

I had read, too, in *The Secret Life of Plants* about the galvanometer experiments that Cleve Backster did with his plants. It seems that in the 1960s in New York City, Backster taught police officers and security agents from around the world to read lie detector tests. As a lark, he began to hook up his own plants to see if they responded to danger. Sure enough, they did. Every plant in Backster's home reacted to just the *thought* of lighting a match under the leaf of one of them, the *Dracaena massangeana*. They even registered emotional reactions to Backster's thoughts when he was many miles away. Once, while he was driving on the New Jersey Turnpike, he sent the thought to his plants that he was coming home. When he arrived, he found that they had responded vigorously on the polygraph, looking forward to seeing him, he surmised.

I took Backster's experiences to heart: I reasoned that if other people could tap some sort of primal sense perception in plants, why couldn't I? It was time to get down to some serious fun with my gardening.

I purposely chose my office as the appropriate place for an initiation into the mysteries of inner gardening. It was a light and airy space, flanked on one wall by a huge south window overlooking the city and on another by a view of the Cathedral of St. John the Divine. A loosely woven blue-and-green wall hanging from Brazil dropped from the ceiling next to my desk, the reds of an Afghan prayer rug vibrated on the hardwood floor, and lots of bushy houseplants made the room look like a conservatory.

I plotted my course while I gathered all the materials I needed, then placed them on some newspaper. I arranged the pot-bound spider plant alongside two new hanging baskets filled with fresh potting soil and set my largest and sharpest kitchen knife next to them. I made sure nobody was home, closed the door for extra privacy, and turned around to face the task. A roaring silence ensued. Now that I had set it up, it was time to follow through.

There didn't seem to be any rules about exactly how to do this sort of thing. I was used to thinking in terms of doing everything "the right way." (Paralyzed by this attitude, I had often ended up doing nothing!) This time was going to be different. I would be brave and forge ahead to make my own way. Isn't that how people discover and invent things?

I took the pot-bound plant in my hands and made my first contact. I tugged hard on the foliage a few times to remind myself how stuck it really was. Maybe it wasn't such a good idea, I thought, pulling on its body like that, but I wanted some sort of acknowledgment between us about its current state.

I focused on the spider plant with both my thoughts and my eyes, giving it my full attention. Then I awkwardly introduced myself. "Hello," I asserted, "I'm Judith, and I want us to become allies so we can work together to separate your root ball into two plants." Strangely enough, I didn't even feel weird. It seemed quite normal to me, so I kept going. I remarked to the spider that it would probably be happier if it had more space and a greater source of nourishment. As things stood now, I added, the spider lived somewhat akin to the wicked stepsister crammed into Cinderella's too-tight slipper. I proposed a better life. Did I make any sense?

I waited for an answer. Nothing happened, so I decided

to proceed. The Findhorn book suggested telling plants what you want to do and why and to be specific. So I let the spider in on my plan. I delineated a straight line across the top of the root ball with the side of my right hand. "This is where I want to cut you in half," I declared. I displayed the knife gingerly, describing to the spider my past attempts at dividing others of its eminent family. I said I wanted to avoid the awful hacking and sawing job that usually occurred when I tried to cut a pot-bound root ball.

I asked the spider to do whatever was necessary to tranquilize and protect itself so it wouldn't pass out and go limp and gray. "Going into shock is no fun," I commiserated. If the spider was amenable to my plan, I'd return in twenty-four hours, and it could demonstrate to me in some way whether I might continue. I set it gently back down on the newspaper, crossed my fingers, and said good-bye. Then I left, carefully and quietly shutting the door behind me.

Once outside the room, I stopped and took a deep breath. It was a propitious moment. I was taking a quantum leap of faith, trusting in the possibility of forces beyond my five senses and asking to receive new insights. I prepared to wait.

As I walked around the house, I became very nervous. I sensed I was on the verge of something new, something that would change me. I didn't know what to expect. Somehow I knew I was invoking help from an invisible source previously untapped.

After a few hours, I couldn't stand it anymore. The suspense was driving me crazy. I was dying to check on the spider plant before the allotted time was up. I knew it wasn't the best thing. My interference might even render the entire experiment null and void. "Nah," I thought, "I'll just peek. It couldn't make *that* big a difference."

So I silently turned the doorknob and tiptoed into the room as if I could fool the plant. If, in fact, it understood more than I previously believed, which was my hypothesis, then it knew very well what I was up to. When I realized this, I gave up my silly charade, walked right up to the plant, and yanked on it. It still wouldn't budge. I felt sheepish, to say the least. It seemed as if the spider was forcing me to wait and follow our original agreement.

I apologized, embarrassed that a grown woman such as myself couldn't wait and uphold her end of such a crucial bargain. I promised the spider that this time I would wait full term.

I fully expected to hear the clock in the Tower of London chime at the appointed hour. Then, with the touch of my magic wand, instead of my carriage turning into a pumpkin, the pumpkin would miraculously split in half and make two. That night I went to bed with great excitement. It was a veritable Christmas Eve.

The next morning, I made sure that I waited until the last second of the twenty-four hours, if for no other reason than for the sake of "science." I boldly opened the door to the operating room and walked in for surgery. I took a deep breath, my heart pounding madly. At the same time, I felt a little silly. What did all this mean, anyway? Part of me wanted to debunk the whole thing. I decided not to allow it and squelched that voice immediately.

I sat down on the floor next to the spider plant. It was then I noticed that the long green leaves had separated of their own accord. Half of them lay to one side of the midpoint, where I had drawn the line with my hand, and the other half lay to the other side, clearly exposing the invisible line. The foliage had actually arranged itself in an orderly fashion as if acknowledging what was about to happen. This in itself was astounding. I took it as an undeniable sign.

I asked the spider if it was ready, thinking I would have to do some tugging and pulling. I lifted the pot and turned it on its side. Before I knew what was happening, the entire root ball, totally intact, plopped right out of the pot. The hairs on my body stood straight up.

I never expected anything like this. Just the day before, the plant had been rigid in its pot with no movement whatsoever. Now it had a mind of its own. It had, literally, jumped onto the floor. I rose to the occasion, picked up the knife, and galvanized my forces for the next stage.

The time had come to cut the root ball in half. I was still skeptical about this part. I mentally relayed my fears to the spider about grinding away at it with the knife and asked for help. Then I steadied my hand, knife poised for the incision, and aimed my attention at the invisible line I had drawn through the middle of the root ball. I lowered the knife and began to cut. When the blade touched the soil, it slid effortlessly, as if by magic, through the myriad roots as if they were made of soft butter.

It was over in a second. "Victory for the forces of good! Here, here!" I cried, jumping up and down, dancing in place, cheering for the spider plant, for our joint effort, and for the wonders of the invisible world I had just entered.

I had a new partner, and it wasn't a silent one either. I gently touched the divided plant and stroked the foliage as if the leaves were Rapunzel's hair. Waves of tenderness washed over me for the plant. Convinced of the validity of my direction, I vowed to finish the project in style.

I relayed thoughts of encouragement to the spider plant, coaxing it to hang on just a little longer while I placed each of its halves in a new pot. I arranged each head of hair, so to speak, attractively in the center of each pot and tamped down the fresh soil to hold the plants in place. I watered each plant well, soaking the soil deeply each time, allowing the water to run out the bottom and watering again and again so no dry spots remained. I knew I could never water too much at one time, only too often, so I didn't stint on water during this climactic part of the transplant.

Although I potted the plants in separate hanging baskets, I hung them closely together in the great south window, the place of honor. There, the sun poured in on them and they adorned this lovely room, illuminating the space with their delicate green glow. I made sure to keep them together. To me, they were like Siamese twins. I thought they'd still appreciate each other's company even after their separation.

The spiders never went into shock, lost their color, or sagged, as other spiders had before. They were perky and vital and unusually lustrous from the very inception of their independent lives. I regarded the three of us as symbolically bonded. We all had survived my first inner gardening experiment.

The spiders helped me harness a secret power that was available simply for the asking. The experiment turned out to be as much about me as it was about the plants. I allowed magic into my life and had opened the way for more to come.

Just in case we lose touch with reality here, I want you to know I have had my share of failures, too. Unwittingly, I began to become attached and limited by my twenty-four-hour-notice time frame. Sometime thereafter, a spineless Medusa cactus set me straight. This unusual plant had long ago outgrown its pot. True to its name, at least thirty gangly arms spread randomly in all directions, like a mass of snakes. The Medusa was so top-heavy, it couldn't stand up without being propped against something for support. Stuck like cement in this too-small pot, the plant wouldn't budge no matter how hard I tugged and pulled. Finally, I gave up and put it down so we could have a conversation.

"Look," I said, "you are living in a pot that is ridiculous for you to remain in any longer. Your roots have displaced all the soil, you have no nourishment, and you can't even stand up. Please release yourself from this pot and let me plant you into a fresh one filled with good soil. Then you'll have plenty of room to grow."

I used my good old twenty-four-hour-notice speech and felt confident that the Medusa would play along. Surely, by this time tomorrow, I could transplant it. But no dice. The next afternoon, it was still not budging. It seemed to be adamant that it wasn't going to move. The day after was the same story, and the day after that, too. I couldn't believe—given my good track record until then and the pitiful condition of its home—that the Medusa was not going to cooperate with me. But I couldn't deny the blatant fact that it had decided to stay in its pot. I insisted I didn't want to break the pot; it seemed too violent. So I said, "Be that way if you want," and haughtily put it aside to stew in its own juices. I went on to other things.

A few weeks passed. I gave up on the plant and shoved it off into a corner of my patio because I was annoyed with it. Its lack of team spirit puzzled me, but I adopted a see-if-I-care attitude. (I wasn't practicing what I preached, but, hey, nobody's perfect.) I went about my other business for the next few weeks, repotting, cleaning, weeding, and generally taking care of everything else in my garden.

One day, when I had finished bringing all the other plants up to optimum, I spotted the Medusa off by itself, sitting in the corner. I glared at it, still a little miffed that it hadn't fit into my twenty-four-hour-notice scenario. I had temporarily forgotten my previous experience and how important it was to cooperate rather than command. It never once dawned on me the plant was doing its best.

I went over to it and said silently, "Okay. Last chance. Do you want to come?" and I gave it a tug, just for the hell of it. Out of the pot it flew, and me with it. Not expecting it to budge, I was thrown off balance, onto my butt. I was floored, and in that instant I realized it had been taking its *own* time, not mine, and I had never even entertained the possibility. Instead, I immediately assumed it was being ornery and uncooperative. This attitude actually says more about me than it does about the plant. We were communicating, after all.

I transplanted the cactus into a clay pot, the size appropriate for a small shrub, and adjusted its stance so its long snake arms could rest on the rim. I played with its appendages, holding them up and feeling the Medusa's energy course through my veins. It seemed like a prehistoric animal to me. What a guy, I kept thinking to myself.

I noted, though, I hadn't planned on putting the Medusa into that large a pot, but as the event unfolded, one I had been reserving for something much taller presented itself strongly. I sat the Medusa inside, and it instantly relaxed its arms on the rim as if it had found its right home. By myself, I never would have thought it needed such a large pot. Once again I learned that if you let it, the process itself, as well as your relationship with the plant, will tell you everything you need to know. Your hand will be guided.

Months later, I moved into a new place with a deck and arranged my succulents together in a grouping in full view of the ocean. The Medusa bloomed. This big gangly, silly-looking plant produced the teensiest red flowers that I ever saw, right on its tips. They appeared in minuscule clusters and measured so small I nearly missed them completely, but their tiny stature made them all the more endearing. The blooms added to the fondness I already felt for the

Medusa. I got to see it give birth. The Medusa had become like family.

My experience with the Medusa reveals the intimacy that develops when you garden with a spiritual philosophy. If you stay open, the plants will teach you. I find this lesson repeats itself over and over again. Here I was, with experience behind me, and I still expected the Medusa to perform on demand. One act of supposed insubordination and what did I do? I blackballed the plant!

When people tell me they have a black thumb and they kill everything they try to grow, no matter how hard they try not to, I know it is because they aren't connecting with the plants. They still view the plants as objects to be manipulated, color to decorate their garden, or something stylish to enhance their living room. It is always a good idea to warm to your plants so they are no longer just things that sit there. Allow that an invisible level of connection actually exists. All that matters is that you have a feeling, or even an idea, of reverence. Thank your plants often and tell them how beautiful they are, how much you love them. Gratitude is a gracious quality to embrace in gardening. Look upon everything you do as another step in creating a sacred space with your garden.

The interconnectedness of all life does not have to be an abstract concept. We can live it. It doesn't matter whether we garden indoors or outdoors; we can honor our world. It's all a prayer. When we act with this attitude, it snowballs and the rewards accrue infinitely. I've seen it happen.

Giving Notice: The Golden Rule of Gardening

> Whenever anyone contributes attention or feeling to
> a plant, a bit of that person's being mingles with a bit
> of our being, and the one world is fostered. You hu-
> mans are therefore all very linked to us, but until you
> give recognition to these links, they are as nothing
> and remain undeveloped.
>
> —The Rhubarb Deva, from *The Findhorn Garden*

In the early seventies, when I worked for NBC All-
News Network Radio, I interviewed the head landscape
gardener at Disneyworld in Orlando, Florida. I wanted
to know if he thought plants could feel or, in some
way, know what was going on. He said yes, and when I
asked him how he knew such a thing, he smiled, know-
ingly. Of all the hundreds of plants, bushes, shrubs, and
trees at Disneyworld, he explained, the ones that died
and had to be replaced the most often were the flowers
(usually impatiens) planted around the benches where
the parents sat and scolded their children. He
adamantly asserted that these plantings shriveled up
and died because of the yelling and screaming and general bad feeling that occurred on those benches.

The experience with my spider plant set me thinking
in a similar direction. I realized I needed to be careful
about how I behaved with my plants. Seemingly, they

understood me and had clearly communicated back. Perhaps not in the same way human beings perceive and talk with one another, but something happened between us that deserved to be examined and pursued.

When I divided my spider, I became aware of what a respectful and considerate policy it is to notify a plant before initiating any major process such as repotting, transplanting, or pruning. Even when preparing new places in the garden that have been wild, or when taking out annuals, for example, it is courteous to ask before simply going in and ripping out plants.

Be with your plants for a while and feel what is going on. Simply observe them. Necessary gardening tasks can be highly intrusive acts to plants, interrupting growth or rest, disrupting places where the fairies live, or breaking apart a growing family. Consider the act of pruning, for example. You know what an emotional issue hair can be. Can you imagine someone suddenly swooping down on you and cutting your hair to a shorter length, or even cutting it off completely without asking first? No kid or cat, adult or dog would sit still for that kind of pruning for long. Plants have no choice. They are firmly rooted and are unable to get up and run away except in cartoons.

Giving notice does not automatically mean the plant will leap out of its pot right away as did my spider. Nothing may happen the first time you give notice. Or, something may happen, but not in the way that you expected. Keep on trying and experimenting.

A plant may need plenty of help from you, such as turning the pot upside down, putting pressure on its sides, cutting the plastic container, or even tugging gently to start the birthing process. Primarily, what giving notice does is set your intent. It aligns you with the plant instead of placing you in opposition to it.

Expecting plants to perform on demand or command is unrealistic. Inner gardening is a more subtle process. As you ease into your indoor or outdoor gardening tasks, put yourself into the plants' shoes, so to speak. Think always how you would feel if you were in the same position, and then you will know what course of action to take.

Let the plant know just what it is you want to do and why. Come from your heart. Do not feel silly or give yourself a hard time because of what others might think about your talking to plants. You are not crazy. You are cooperating with other living beings and creating a bridge of communication between you and your garden, your world, your planet, and your own heart.

Address the plant silently or speak out loud, depending on how you feel most at ease. I usually feel more authentic and able to express myself more clearly and freely when I communicate through thought rather than audibly, with words. The most important element, though, is the purity of your intent. You are cultivating love and compassion, a sensitivity to life and the ability to see its miracles. This attitude will translate itself to all living things through your actions and the type of care you give.

Building this bridge is a happy and innocent task. Do not inhibit your behavior by worrying that you are not doing it correctly. There is no such thing as "the right way." You are finding the right way for you. Inner gardening is about thinking for yourself, being yourself, and then watching the results flower around you.

Trust your instincts and your intuitions. Listen to your inner voice. When that intuitive voice comes giving you an answer, listen to it. We all have experiences in life of hearing that voice and then not trusting it. We ignore it and figure out a rational solution. Later we discover we should have listened. What the small voice said was correct—and it was the first thing that came to mind.

When I become aware that I have shunned my intuition, I usually berate myself and swear I won't do it again. But, I often do. It takes a lot of practice to go with the nonrational. Western society does not support such "nonsense." But inner gardeners can change this kind of linear thinking. Use your gardening tasks as an opportunity to encourage and heed your intuitive voice. It will create a domino effect in other areas of your life. Perhaps the next time you hear your inner voice say that the baby-sitter isn't trustworthy or your date isn't a good match for you, you will give it more credence. Then, later on, you won't have to say, "I knew that. I should have listened to myself."

Once you have established a relationship with your plants, you will feel more connected with them. Something will happen that is hard to describe. It is the same feeling you get for the ones you love. You want to do the right thing for them, you want to please them, you want to protect them.

THREE

Petunias and
My Inner Worth

Earth has no sorrow that earth cannot heal.

—John Muir, *John of the Mountains*, 1938

Petunias had never been one of my favorite flowers. As a matter of fact, I didn't even like them until they won my attention in an odd, fortuitous sort of way. Then they became more than just color to enliven my garden; petunias emphatically planted themselves in my heart.

When we arrive at the setting of this story, I was just turning twenty-eight and my marriage was dying. On the surface we were the perfect couple. Or, so everyone thought. We chose to live a lie. We never discussed our unhappiness together. Now the time had come to struggle with an issue I never thought I would have to face. I was pregnant and petrified.

In our society, or probably any society for that matter, women who don't want babies are looked upon with disdain, disbelief, and pity. They are often considered selfish, lacking the motherly instinct to raise another human being. I grappled with that stereotype for a while, feeling guilty and ostracized by my own acceptance of it. Then my panic took over, my nauseating fear and morning sickness that lasted morning, noon, and night. Everything overwhelmed me. I finally admitted to myself that I did not want to bear this child, that I wanted to have an abortion.

Even though I was twenty-eight years old, I was extraordinarily ignorant. I didn't have the slightest idea as to *when* a woman could have an abortion. How much time did I have? When would I be forced to admit to the world what I really wanted to do?

I owned a pirated copy of *Our Bodies, Ourselves* by the Boston Women's Collective, in those days a radical tract. I had never touched the mimeographed pages stashed away in my drawer, saved from my student days at the University of Wisconsin at Madison. After all, I prided myself on how well I took care of my gynecological needs. I had a Pap smear and an internal examination every year, didn't I? And I was a pioneer user of birth control pills in high school.

"What a joke," I thought. I didn't know anything. It was time to read the book.

I could scarcely breathe as I turned the pages. I discovered I needed to decide by the twelfth *week*. If I waited beyond that time, I would need to be injected with a saline solution and have to go through the birth process, giving birth to a dead fetus. That was too close for me. Too close to the truth of what I was actually going to do. At least with an early abortion, they would put me out cold.

Ashamed that I didn't have the slightest idea of how to take care of a baby, let alone love it, I couldn't confide my terror to anyone. The underlying panic persisted that I would surely have an emotionally out of control kid because I felt that way inside. I was not mother material.

The level of deceit I lived while trying to find a way out was appalling. Unfortunately, my husband and I had already told everybody the supposedly wonderful news. Everyone was happy for us. So I performed like an actor in a play, on the outside, and lived another completely alien life on the inside. Tormented by every demon of negative emotion that exists within the human heart, I carried on a constant dialogue with myself about what I might do and how I would do it. My time was running out. It was the end of April and I had until the beginning of June. My one saving grace, though, was that I was a lost soul and I knew it. I sincerely wanted to do the right thing. But I feared reproach from those who watched, and I hated myself and judged myself more harshly than any onlooker probably ever did.

My husband and I rented a place in the country for our weekly escape from the rigors of life in Manhattan. Every Friday afternoon we would load the car, which was parked all week long at the local garage on 113th Street and Broadway, and propel ourselves in a none-too-relaxed fashion to the joys of country living. When we got there, we'd unpack, go food shopping for the weekend, cook endless meals, and wash umpteen dishes. Then on Sunday night, we'd pack up again, including all the uneaten food, and drive back to "Rome," back to the hell of a declining civilization.

The house, circa 1860, was made of stone and wood. I had

to bend over slightly to clear the doorway into the living room. The couple we rented it with were our best friends. The wife was having trouble getting pregnant and wanted babies so badly it consumed her. I felt guilty because I was pregnant and secretly didn't want to have the child. I wished I could have given her my baby and everyone would have been happy.

On this particular Memorial Day weekend, we arrived in the country to open the house for the summer. The water that ran in the house smelled like sulfur. When I took a shower, brushed my teeth, or washed the dishes, I ended up gagging or vomiting, sensitive to the odor because I was pregnant.

For distraction on Saturday morning, I decided to go to the local nursery and look at the flowers for sale. When I arrived at the nursery, the only nice-looking sets left were of petunias. Petunias were not my first choice. I wasn't crazy about picking off their dead heads all the time to keep them looking good, a need even more peculiar to the petunia than other flowers, I believed. But, of all the flowers on sale, the petunias were the freshest and healthiest. I chose an assortment of three: deep violet, a smoldering magenta, and pure white. There was something inside me that was driving me to plant. I had to plant that day.

I drove home, all the while glancing at the petunias to make sure they were all right. It was hot that day, and I didn't want them to droop beyond the point of no return before I even got them home. I carried the box to the back of the house and began to search for a spot to plant them. The area was covered with grass. There didn't seem to be a patch of dirt anywhere.

"Ah, there's a spot," I said with relief. Right out the back door sat an old tree stump. It wasn't a big stump, but the dirt all around it could be turned and planted. I began to dig deeply with my hand trowel and prepare the way for my new acquaintances, the petunias.

I admired them thoughtfully, holding up each little potted flower as I poked around for buds in their various stages of unfoldment. I was pleased, I decided. I had chosen well. They were fine specimens and my favorite colors, too: violet, magenta, and white.

Slowly and carefully, I began to dig a place for them in the ground. I arranged them with an artist's eye, becoming blissfully lost in the process. The petunias looked exquisite when I finished watering them. Their colors glowed like the velvets on a Renaissance palette. Those petunias almost transcended their genus and species. They were the blueprint for all petunias everywhere. They didn't have any brown or yellow leaves or crunchy, dried-up flowers. They were the most luscious petunias I had ever seen before or since.

After I finished and cleaned up my planting mess, I was rudely catapulted back into the excruciating reality in which I lived. Some relatives were on the phone to congratulate us on the pregnancy. Once again, I was faced with a baby inside me that I was terrified to have. I hadn't told another human being, even my therapist, of my fear. In those days, I kept everything hidden, afraid to tell another person the truth because then I would have to act on it.

I still didn't know what I was going to do. How was I going to straighten out my warped existence and not hurt anybody? How was I going to save myself? I climbed the creaky stairs to the whitewashed room I shared with my husband. He had built us a bed underneath a little window in the stone wall so we could hear the stream rush past. As I huddled in bed under the quilt, the cool night air soothed me. Ironically, the quilt belonged in a child's room blocked out with little girls with giant curls hidden under hats that covered their faces.

When I finally fell asleep, I dreamed I was walking in the woods on a carpet of moss. Spongy and wet, it sunk under my feet like quicksand. Soon I came to a clearing. The light changed to the kind of light that gleams around four o'clock on winter afternoons. It cast a pink-and-orange otherworldly glow over everything. The light helped me see into the plants, into the natural world, and sense magic.

It was there, in the black humus of the forest, that I saw the white petunias. They stood in profusion, very close together, and they were talking to me. It was almost as if each petunia had a face and a voice and a personality. I heard them say in unison, "Hello, Judith. You planted our seed. Please help us to grow."

When I awoke the next morning, I remembered the dream so intensely it seemed as if it had actually happened. I had the feeling that I had just been given an answer to my prayers but it wasn't clear yet what it was. It had come in a form in which I would have to decide for myself what it meant.

Many people, I realize, might have interpreted the dream differently than I did. In the end, I decided that the petunias in the dream were the deepest part of me. I had planted my own seed of consciousness and I needed to help it grow, no matter what it took to make that happen, even if it meant having an abortion for reasons of mental and emotional incapability. I didn't know why at the time, but I needed to have an abortion so I could live. I thought I was a terrible person for feeling this way and I wished things were different, but at least I was telling the truth.

So one night, as we lay together under the little girls' quilt, I told my husband that I wanted to have an abortion. I said that I loved him, but there was only friction left in our marriage and I was terrified to have a baby. I needed help. We needed help. Telling him was the hardest thing I ever did. And my husband did not respond well.

In fact, he called me a dried-up, shriveled old witch and left me right on the spot. He took his socks and underwear out of our drawers and went down to the station to wait for the next train to the city. For the first time since I found out I was pregnant, I took a deep breath.

At the therapist's office the following week, my husband said he would stay with me if I went through with having the baby. I told him I wanted him to stay because he wanted to be with me. We didn't work it out. I went through with the abortion. I repeated the name of God over and over until the sodium Pentothal did its work and put me out. When I awoke, I hurt everywhere, particularly in my heart. I could hardly believe all this was happening to me.

My mother couldn't stay away from the abortion clinic. I hadn't wanted her to come. But she arrived in time to help me home in a cab and put me to bed. She stayed with me for the first night, hovering and fretting, worried about my condition. I just wanted her to back off and let me be.

The next morning the obligatory New York cock-roaches were crawling all over my kitchen because I had abandoned my post there for a couple of days. My original deal with them was they could live there and I wouldn't use the Raid if they didn't show their faces while I was in the kitchen. If they did, I would be forced to kill them.

We had achieved this typical New York détente during the time I was home to converse with them. Now, they became shameless and broke our tentative bargain. They were brazenly running across the counters and all over the tile floor. My mother had bought a can of bug spray and was determinedly spraying it everywhere. I ran into the kitchen and started screaming at her to stop killing the cockroaches.

"I have a deal with them!" I yelled.

She looked at me as if I were nuts. Suddenly, I broke down sobbing with the horrible realization that I was losing it over the cockroaches but had just had an abortion the day before. How perverse could life get? I was at a complete loss.

Days, weeks, months passed. I was guilty and confused and so afraid about what people would say that I told everyone I had lost the baby. I lied, ashamed of my choice to abdicate motherhood. It took many years before I was able to mourn and grieve for the child and resolve the pain of what I had done. I had to struggle with my own ambivalence and the paradoxical nature of the situation. I made the right decision in order to save myself, but I needed forgiveness for my choice. In the end, I was the only one who could bestow it.

My husband and I separated, and I continued to work with my business partner in our indoor-outdoor gardening service. Functioning like a sleepwalker, dutifully I went to the addresses of our business accounts and watered and pruned the plants. It was a good therapeutic job for me. I was running on automatic.

For the public rooftop gardens at a major New York publisher, the flower boxes needed to look good. So, we planted giant yellow and orange marigolds up and down the whole length of their outdoor terrace overlooking midtown Manhattan. I went twice a week to water and weed. The marigolds began to grow.

Each time I came to water, I would examine the whole city block's worth of marigold boxes by fishing around in the soil to make sure there were no bugs. One day, as I poked around in the marigolds, something strange happened that miraculously jolted me back to my inner truth. The box of marigolds at the very end of the line was filled with sprouting petunias.

I lowered my head to get a closer look, tilting it sideways as I stared in disbelief. Petunias, growing where no petunias had been planted. I kept thinking, I must be wrong. I asked my partner, but she hadn't planted them, either. There must be a logical explanation. As they grew, I couldn't deny their reality. In a few weeks, the box at the end of the terrace was blooming with violet, magenta, and white petunias.

They were blooming for me. They were letting me know I hadn't been wrong. They hadn't abandoned me. In the midst of my pain, they were acknowledging the courage of my decision. Even though I had misgivings about what I had to do, I had known what was best for me and my unborn child. There was no choice but the one I chose. And the petunias knew it.

For a long time, just seeing petunias reminded me of that dark period in my life. Now they have taken their proper place in perspective. They were my first partners in inner knowing. I listened to them and trusted their message. At the time, they were my only light.

In retrospect, the petunia incident was part of a larger lesson about nurturing. Before seed can germinate, the ground has to be prepared; before I could nurture a child properly, I needed to nurture and grow myself. A first step, for me, was to acknowledge my own stunted level of growth. Having a woman's body and physical capabilities wasn't enough. I needed some emotional grounding and maturity, too.

After my petunia episode, I finally made my trip to Findhorn, my first spiritual pilgrimage. I flew to Glasgow as part of a group that attended a three-week global conference at the Findhorn Community. Upon arrival in Glasgow, we boarded a bus for an eight-hour ride north to the tip of Scotland. As we drove through miles and miles of national forest, my anticipation grew.

Our first group meeting, in a large circular hall still under construction, united hundreds of people from all over the world to attend numerous workshops on gardening, spirituality, and our relationship to the earth. After the introductory talks, people shared garden experiences that were as meaningful to them as mine were to me. We exchanged information and points of view, developed camaraderie, and built support for those of us who felt out of touch with any sense of community like this at home.

I learned at Findhorn that my treatment of garden tools was as important as my attitude toward the plants. I needed to keep the tools clean and well oiled so rust wouldn't form. Putting them back in the shed when I finished using them assured their longevity. If I respected the tools and allowed them to do the work, they would.

For example, rather than my being tense and forcing my action on the hoe, they suggested holding the hoe loosely and relaxing into the rhythm, allowing the hoe to move me. Oddly enough, it worked. The technique presented a new awareness about allowing rather than imposing. When I applied the principle to other parts of my life, I discovered I needed to let go and let life unfold rather than try so hard to control it.

Life at Findhorn was decidedly less serious than I had imagined. Eileen and Peter Caddy invited us all to partake at the Findhorn Pub after the evening's activity. After a hard day in the garden or giving service somewhere else in the community, people had a good time dancing, drinking, and talking. Even though I didn't drink, my rigid ideas about what was "spiritual" faded fast. An embrace of life rather than a rejection of it was the example they set.

We were taught to respect the process of life, to respect everything we did, whether we were washing dishes, cleaning toilets, or running the front desk. Whatever we were doing had value and served a purpose. I myself did not immediately grasp the depth of this concept, I was so busy worrying. One day I had been asked to file cards in the office. Humdrum and boring compared to my expectations, the job's one saving grace was the view I had of people working, laughing, and talking in the garden. It looked like fun, and I felt sorry for myself cooped up in an office doing unglamorous work. Since everyone got to try different jobs, I didn't last long at mine.

I didn't learn the lesson until many years later that it

wasn't what I did, but how I did it, that mattered. I would notice how good I felt when an anonymous telephone operator treated me with kindness or a waiter was genuinely interested in serving me well. I began to see how little it takes to share loving-kindness with others and to do it even in the seemingly mundane tasks of the day. If I could do it with plants, I could do it with people, too.

This truth still comes to me through gardening. Plants are my company and my solace, my friends and my refuge. When all else fails, I go to them to regain my center. My plants help me to love myself with the same care and respect I give to them.

Gardening nourishes; it refreshes, revitalizes, replenishes, and restores. My mother always says that Mozart is better than any psychiatrist. I feel the same way about plants.

I can even imagine planting petunias again someday.

Growing the Kids

> I want to know God's thoughts ... the rest are details.
>
> —Albert Einstein

My time to be involved with children came many years later. After I wrote a children's book, I began to visit classrooms and plant indoor gardens with children. My goal was to incorporate the spiritual aspects of gardening into teaching children about plants.

As part of a community project by the Decorative Arts Study Center, I was invited to speak to a second-grade class in San Juan Capistrano, California. We planted garlic cloves to grow garlic-tasting scallions, the crown of a pineapple for a pretty succulent plant (and with luck a blue flower and a miniature pineapple), and a few yams so their pretty purple and green vines would grow long and the kids could follow their growth, winding them around the classroom.

As I began the project, I asked the children, "Who in this class likes attention?" Of course, everyone raised their hands including the teachers, the parents, and me. I told them everything alive loves attention. The more attention you give to plants, the happier they will be. I emphasized that the most important thing to put into a garden is love.

Each child's face relaxed. Their shoulders dropped and big smiles appeared. Suddenly, we weren't doing a dry science project anymore. Their hearts were involved.

Later, I told them I believed there were flower fairies and asked them if they did, too. I wanted to see what they thought. I was surprised at their animated response. Many of the kids had concrete questions for the flower fairies, such as What do you eat? Where do you sleep? Do you go to school? The teacher asked everyone to paint a picture of a flower fairy and write directly to the fairies with their questions.

At the end of the class, a long line formed with all

the kids who wanted to tell me their stories. As I sat
with them and listened, they draped themselves over
me and excitedly shared tales about their favorite plants
at home. Sparking their love had transformed science
into magic.

The class happened in spring. In June, as a continua-
tion of the outreach program, I joined with other members of the Decorative Arts Study Center in hosting a
year-end celebration in their Children's Garden. When
this class arrived, their teacher bragged to me that the
kids were actually vying with each other for the opportunity to water the indoor garden we planted. They
had an enthusiasm for the garden, eager to show who
cared about it most.

Our team laminated the watercolors the kids
painted of the flower fairies and hung them among the
trees and shrubs in the Children's Garden. We distrib-
uted handwritten answers to their letters on parch-
ment scrolls sprinkled with glitter and tied with gold
ribbon. The kids went wild opening their individual-
ized answers.

One boy huddled in a corner looking very upset.
When I went up to him and asked what was wrong, he
said he hadn't received his answer. I promised him I'd
look around for the scroll. Perhaps it had gotten lost. I
hurried into the office and wrote him a note, signing it,
the Garlic, Yam, and Pineapple Fairies. These were the
same recycled kitchen scraps we had planted in his
classroom. In the letter, I reminded him to put love into
his garden and thanked him for the kind care he gave
the plants. Then I added, "We love you." At first I wondered if this was too sappy for a boy, but then some-

thing inside me said to let it go. I wrapped the scroll
with gold ribbon and hurried outside waving the letter,
pretending I had just found it. "The fairies must have
dropped it on their way," I said, handing it to him tri-
umphantly.

His face lit up, and he quietly opened the scroll and
read the contents. I eavesdropped when he rushed over
to a group of boys gathered together away from the
other children. Pointing to the last line, he confided,
"Look, the fairies say they love me. Don't tell anyone.
Okay?" The other boys nodded respectfully.

Nurturing, caring, and respect are easy to cultivate
through gardening, even in children. It is a natural
arena in which children can respond with an open heart
if you encourage them to do so. That day at the study
center I asked all the children to close their eyes and
feel their heart. "Remember how you feel when you really love your dog or your cat, your best friend, or your
mommy and your daddy and they love you back? You
can reach the fairies anytime if you go to that place in
your heart. That's where the fairies live."

The kids fell silent and still, squeezing their eyes
shut, trying to concentrate. When we opened our eyes,
it took a while for the noise and excitement to build
again. The children had actually focused inside so they
could feel their own love and it took them some time to
come out again.

Perhaps, we've gone too far over to one side, relegating science to the realm of the rational and provable,
eliminating the magic and mystery from it. Maybe now
the pendulum will swing back, toward the marriage of
science and poetry. That means reintroducing myth

and fairy tale, dreams and visions, intuition and imagination as spiritually valid ways to understand nature.

When I visit classrooms, I am surprised to discover how many children spend time in or under trees for a sense of comfort and belonging. The kids relate to trees and gardens as safe places to be. Plants are their friends.

One fourth-grade boy told me how he loved a special oak tree that lived behind his house. He said he climbed the tree when his sister beat him up and was mean to him. The oak was the only tree in the yard his sister could not climb. It was too big. He would stay in that tree for hours, it felt so good up there. One day he came home from school to find the tree had been cut down. He missed it. Now there was no place he could go to escape from his sister.

In a fifth-grade class on Earth Day, a boy raised his hand and said that he heard when a tree is cut down, all the other trees around it harden in response. A girl in the same class shared that she loved a big shrub in her mother's garden. She had developed a relationship with it and was sad to come home from school one day to see it gone. Her mother told her she had decided it was too big for the garden, and had asked the gardener to take it away. This child loved the shrub. She had developed a rich fantasy life around it, and this spot had become her favorite place to play. Her comment: "I guess my mother didn't know it was my friend. She didn't even ask me whether she could pull it out or not." I suggested the girl ask her mother to give her a place in the garden that she could call her own and to please consult her if she wants to do anything to it.

Children understand the world of plants. The concept of fairies, not necessarily tiny people with wings but an intelligence within nature, is natural to them.

Give children a spot in the garden that is theirs, where they have dominion, especially children who show a penchant for planting. Instilling in a child love and reverence for life and the earth means giving the child love and respect. Buying rain forest T-shirts is all well and good, but the child needs to know he or she is connected to the earth wherever that child is, even indoors with plants in a city apartment.

Do not hesitate to incorporate fairy tales, storytelling, and myths into gardening with kids. I tell them that fairies flourish in a garden, especially if you make them welcome. All this means is acknowledging their presence. The fairies live in places that are very quiet. When you look there, it is often overgrown, and you might have the feeling not to disturb that area.

In a garden I once renovated, one spot, off in a corner, I felt as though I should never dig or plant there. Vines and weeds covered the place, and I had a healthy respect for the sense of privacy I felt emanating from its core. To me, it was the wild spot in the garden where the fairies lived.

One day, my landlady, Miriam, and her boyfriend, Doug, came over to inspect what I had done. Before I knew it, Miriam started ripping out this weed-strewn place to clean it up. Doug told her stop and leave it alone. "It looks natural," he proclaimed. He may not have thought fairies lived there, but he sensed the wildness of the spot and wanted to preserve it. Be sensitive

to the need of every garden to have its wild spot.
Watch for the wild spot in your garden. There is one.

Loving the earth is a global and overwhelming task.
Healing ourselves is where we begin. My friend Deborah and her three-year-old son, Jazz, planted unpopped popcorn in pots following the directions from one of the projects in my children's gardening book. When I told him that American Indians liked to sing up the corn, it captured his imagination.

One day when I visited, Jazz took me by the hand and proudly showed me what he was doing. He had placed the pots, of growing corn next to his bed on the night table. He liked to sleep with the plants for company. He pointed to each plant and told me a story related to their growth. Deborah said she used to hear him singing to the corn in the morning before he got out of bed. "Good morning, corn. Singing the corn. Sing, sing, sing."

Kids respond to love and fairies, love and attention, love and more love. We are all kids. If you make the garden a science experiment, make sure you add the proven ingredient: human love. Everything thrives on it here in the realm of matter.

The Ficus Tree and My Divorce

We began
as a mineral. We emerged
into plant life
and into animal state, and then into
being human,
and always we have forgotten
our former states, except in early spring, when we
slighty recall
being green again.

—Jelaluddin Rumi, Persian mystic poet,
thirteenth century

The ficus tree came into our lives unexpectedly. It happened in the sixteenth-floor apartment in which the spider and I made contact and overlapped with the decline of my marriage and our eventual divorce. Spacious, with plenty of double windows overlooking the city, the apartment had a pretty view at night because of the lights. From the living room, you could look down Broadway and see an electric path of iridescent ribbon that stretched circuitously toward midtown. You also couldn't see the soot.

Being up so high, with no other tall buildings close by, I could see lots of sky, something unusual in Manhattan. I watched the clouds roll by and the weather systems move in and out. I lived closer to the elements here in this apartment than in any other place I had ever dwelled.

Outside the kitchen window, the top of the Cathedral of St. John the Divine loomed nearby. The angel Gabriel flew above blowing his horn, and with his golden weathered patina, resembled a Christmas card you'd buy at the Metropolitan Museum of Art gift shop. When I stared at him, wondering what I was doing living in the city when I longed for green countryside, he gave me heart.

Ensconced in my sunny urban kitchen, I baked bread and put up pickles and pretended I lived in the country. I arranged all my grains and beans in glass jars on the shelves so I could see them and identify each one by color and shape and not need labels. And houseplants continued to be my substitute for country living.

I grew all the common varieties of indoor plants, the greenhouse tropicals that were in vogue at the time. I was particularly fond of the furry hanging rabbit's foot fern in my study and the false aralia, looking very Chinese pagodalike, in the hall. When I was home alone, I communed with my plants. I didn't think. I didn't worry. I lived totally in the moment, watering and pruning, spraying and washing, repotting and overseeing. I arranged the plants in combinations and displays that showed them off to their best advantage. In short, I gave them direct and focused attention.

One day, I met my business partner at a potential account in a fancy law office in lower Manhattan. In the middle of the reception area stood a giant *Ficus benjamina* in a custom-built, high-tech chrome container. Stoically greeting everyone who entered, it was discreetly illuminated by spotlights from within a false ceiling. Theoretically, the tree was supposed to thrive. In reality, the poor thing was dying. There was not enough light to keep a philodrendron alive, let alone a sun-loving ficus.

Yellow leaves fluttered to the floor as we spoke, lending an autumnal effect to the severity of the office space. Since it wasn't fall and we were indoors, the look lacked charm. No longer appropriate for welcoming new clients, the ficus tree needed to be replaced with something more upbeat.

My partner and I removed the tree from its grave and placed it into our truck. It was then I noticed the ficus was covered with scale. I sat next to it, thinking twice about throwing it away. It had reached seven feet high and five feet wide—and was a major ordeal to move. We had no idea what to do with it. It seemed a shame to dump it, but what was the alternative?

We left it in the truck while we made our rounds, and later my partner said, "If *you* don't want it, it's history."

So, I went home that night and began to seriously consider taking the tree home. I felt as if I were adopting a child. And a child with a handicap, at that.

I sat in our living room and stared at the space. The tree would fill about a quarter of the room. But, if I placed it in between the two south windows that faced down Broadway, it would fit in nicely. I imagined the ficus tree sitting there in good health, diverting light as the sun streamed in. In my vision, having the tree would be like living in the country, looking out at the world from inside a wood. Just imagining it made me relax.

Living on the sixteenth floor was noisy. I noticed that I could hear conversations clearly from the street, not to mention the sirens and the horns. Sometimes I couldn't even hear the stereo when the noise level reached particularly high decibels. Perhaps my solution had just presented itself. Maybe a big tree in the room might absorb some of the sound. It worked that way in nature. I'd soothe my raw nerves immersed in a self-made forest while the city traffic screeched below.

I arranged to have the tree brought to the house. It had to be delivered in the service elevator, since it was too big to travel with the passengers. Then it had to be scrunched through two doorways in order to reach the open living room.

Having its branches pressed closely together to avoid breakage must have been hard on the tree. Pressed and pushed, tilted and banged, then almost dropped, I cringed for the ficus as we took it through its paces.

At last we plunked it down in its rightful spot, the one I had envisioned the night before during my planning reveries. Perfect fit, as if it had always been waiting for this place on the planet. The crown of the tree almost touched our eight-foot ceiling. I quickly arranged all my smaller plants around it, creating a skirtlike effect as one would around a Christmas tree. I pushed together all the ferns and dracaenas, parlor palms and spiders, spathiphyllum and pothos to fashion a bank of green under the umbrella of this imposing tree.

The ficus had arrived safely and survived the journey. Now I was going to have to rejuvenate it. But suddenly I saw it for what it really was. Bare. What looked like a deciduous tree in winter was sitting in the middle of my living room. It wasn't, to the unloving eye, what you'd call beautiful.

I devoted myself to the task of bringing it back. My husband and I had bought a hammock in the Yucatán the year before. I found myself thinking it would be a kick to swing in the hammock under a tree in my own living room. So I decided the time was now to act out my fantasy of living in the country and set to work.

I enlisted the aid of my husband, and we installed giant metal hooks onto the side walls of the apartment. We slung our Mexican hammock across the living room under the ficus tree with no leaves, and I got the sense of water I wanted from the sweet smell of earth wafting from the pot after I soaked the soil, my version of spring rain.

For weeks I tried to get rid of the scale. First, I swabbed it off with cotton and alcohol. Then I made a mixture of soap and water and sprayed the entire tree, wiping the leaves with a sponge. Tiny pieces of brown rubbed off, but not enough to make a difference. Then I tried to pick off the scale with my fingers. That was disgusting. The scale that remained was so persistent, I couldn't budge any of it. Sadly, I sprayed with toxic chemicals. I didn't know what else to do. Even that didn't work. Finally, I succumbed to the dreaded systemic-in-the-soil routine. (These pesticides are absorbed into the tissues of plants and become poisonous to parasites that feed on them.) I felt awful doing it, and that didn't work either. The scale was firmly entrenched.

From then on, I realized that if the ficus tree wanted to live, it was going to have to do so in spite of the scale. The two needed to achieve an ecological détente. They had to coexist. I let go of trying to save the plant and told the tree it was going to have to take responsibility for its own life. I would water it and clean its leaves, spray it once in a while to simulate rain, give it fresh air and generally love it, but the rest it would have to do itself. With this understanding, our symbiotic relationship began.

I spent hours under the ficus tree. It gave me infinite pleasure to stretch out in my hammock and look up into the branches, getting to know every inch. The tree was a stalwart presence in the living room and in my life. It depended on me for basic care, and I depended on it for companionship.

One day, in my travels, I found a tiny, perfectly crafted abandoned bird's nest. I didn't know enough about birds to know what kind of nest it was. Even so, it was just the right thing to put in my tree. I brought it home and started poking around looking for exactly the right spot. Eventually the perfect place made itself known. I nestled it into a secure position on the bough so it wouldn't fall. A good friend donated a tiny red cardinal made out of some natural fiber that looked rustic enough to put into the nest, and voilà . . . a total ecosystem. Tree, plants, bird, nest, leaves, branches, hammock, and human. The only thing missing was rushing water, and I provided that with my imagination. I stood back to admire my faux forest. It felt as real to me as any place in nature.

This romance continued for a long time: a full year, at least. At some point, the branches began to bud. The tree bloomed with sweet, tender, green shoots that seemed all the more beautiful juxtaposed to the bare branches. So delicate was the color, so vibrant the effect, sometimes I even forgot that I was indoors. It became springtime inside even when it snowed outside.

The ficus came back with a flourish. It grew healthy and strong despite the fact that it still had as much scale on it as the day I had brought it home. Their truce had worked. Everyone got to live. I became the ficus tree's biggest fan.

During the time I poured all this energy into my garden, my husband and I grew further apart. You might ask, with some justice, "Why didn't she pour all this love into him?" Well, all I can say is, I did the best I could at the time. Neither of us seemed to know how to love each other in the ways we needed to be loved. No matter how hard we tried, nothing worked. Even though we both spoke English, we never understood what the other one was saying.

After we separated, I lived alone in that big apartment for about six months. I was so immature at the time, I had no concept of what had happened. It felt as if I had been whirling around helplessly inside a vortex that propelled me into a certain action. There had been a big emotional explosion and, suddenly, my life was in a shambles. I wanted to retrace my steps but it was too late. I had to learn to live with the consequences of what had occurred.

When I felt ready, I began to look for a smaller and cheaper place to live. Eventually, I found an affordable apartment in an old brownstone on West 90th Street. The one-bedroom wonder had ten-foot ceilings but not much floor space. There was no way the ficus tree would fit.

For a long time, I couldn't even face the possibility of parting company with it. Would you be able to sell, or even give away, your beloved cat or precious dog to a stranger? Finally I stopped denying the inevitable. I had to figure out what to do. I decided to ask my mother if she would take the tree. She had a sunny spot for it in her dining room. Then I could still see the ficus whenever I went over for dinner, like visitation rights or joint custody. Luckily, she agreed to take it as soon as I needed to move.

The ficus would need to go through many difficult transitions to get out of my house, down the elevator, into the truck, across Manhattan, into another delivery entrance, up the elevator, and into my mother's house. When viewed in those terms, I realized how much it would have to endure in order to arrive in one piece and maintain its equilibrium.

The day before I moved, I realized I had been putting off too long facing the ficus tree directly. Boxes were everywhere. The hammock was down and packed. I realized then that I had been mourning the end of my marriage through the tree. The boundary between it and my husband blurred. The giant hooks on the walls remained as the only sign of our time together.

I took a deep breath and readied myself to let the ficus know what was going to happen the next day and why. This approach had worked with the spider plant, so I decided to give it a try with the tree. I went into the living room and drew close to the ficus. I held a leafy branch in both hands, gently making direct contact with it, as one might "breathe" with a horse. I talked silently with my thoughts.

"You must know what's going on," I communicated. "You live here. You probably know the story even better than I do."

I paused for a moment, wanting to be as authentic as possible. Then I continued, "It's time for you to move tomorrow. I'm sorry I can't keep you with me. It's impossible, even though I really want you to come. My new home is too small. I'm giving you to my mother because she has enough space, and then I'll be able to see you when I visit her. I'd like you to do whatever is necessary so you can be moved in peace and you will survive it without going into shock."

Once I had begun, I realized I had more to say. I found myself adding, "Thank you for the pleasure you gave me during our time together. I loved taking care of you and watching you grow." I remained with the tree for a long time in silence. Then I touched it gently to complete the contact and left. I felt like I was losing my best friend.

Later, some relatives took me out to dinner. When I got home, I was tired and a little apprehensive about the next day. Everything would change. I walked into the house, through the long foyer and past the living room. I glanced absentmindedly at the tree in the darkened room. I was so sleepy, I just kept walking down the hallway to the bedroom.

I began to undress and sat down on the bed. It was then I saw something unusual out of the corner of my eye. I turned, and there on the night table, perfectly centered and very green, was one leaf from the ficus tree.

At first I thought, this is impossible. It must have blown into the bedroom with the wind. But there was no wind and there were no other leaves. The ficus tree was far away, down the hall, around a corner and across the living room.

Everything hit me at once. I lay on my bed, clutching the ficus leaf in my hands, and I cried until I fell asleep.

Who Wants to Come? The Etiquette of Picking

> I just come and talk to the plants, really—very important to talk to them; they respond, I find.
>
> —Prince Charles

There is an etiquette or code I have come to apply
with great care whenever I pick or prune anything. First,
I ask, "Who wants to come?" Asking this question engages
the plant in an exchange and offers it a choice. In

nature, before I pick a flower or cut a small piece of
branch from a shrub or a tree, I ask the same question.
Then I pull lightly on the branch to see if it comes easily.
If it doesn't, I go on to another and ask the same question.

The ones who want to come break off readily and
easily at the slightest touch. As soon as I feel resistance, I
know it has not volunteered. When I approach a plant
with a pruner, I scan the plant first and feel which of its
parts are ready to come. I sense it. To do this well, I allow myself a few moments of stillness and quiet in which
to align with the plant. This attitude sets up a more sensitive link with the plant and affords an increased level of
intuitive direction before going in and just cutting.

The technique works for flower picking, pruning,
fruit picking, vegetable harvesting, and for taking cuttings. It is a compassionate way to deal with plants and
an acknowledgment of them offering themselves to you
for food or decoration.

In my effort to try to keep my greed under control,
asking who wants to come insures I don't pick too
much. Sometimes in my haste to cut back a plant or remove dead material, I break off a flower or a good
chunk of stem. Saying you are sorry can help keep your
focus. It is a good reminder to slow down, pay attention, be present. Nothing alive likes to feel that its own
little niche of space in the universe has been invaded.
Offering a please or a thank you respects the living
presence of the plant.

When you pick flowers, fruits, or vegetables, or groom,
prune, transplant, water, or weed your plants, give appreciation. Even after getting up from under the shade of a
tree, saying thank you is a way of reminding yourself that

there has been an exchange. Thank your plants whenever you can. This acknowledgment makes you more receptive to those states of grace in which it is made known to you that you have been given a gift from a plant.

Asking "Who wants to come?" when I shop for plants at the nursery works, too. I leave it up to the plants to designate who wants to come and then wait to feel their pull when I look at them. This intuitive approach works for me. At the same time, I use my discrimination.

If the plant looks sickly, droopy, limp, or discolored, it doesn't come home with me. I am not the Mother Teresa of gardening. On the other hand, if a friend gives me a plant in poor condition and I really like it, I will take it home and try to bring it back to health.

If you are buying plants at a nursery, consider the ones that are bouncy, vibrant, appealing, and bushy and that radiate a healthy-looking color. Forget leggy, scrawny, yellow, brown, crispy, splotchy, and downtrodden unless, of course, salvaging plants is your thing, in which case it's okay.

In the past, I have had very good luck taking plants that have been thrown out behind supermarkets and bringing them back to life. Sometimes you can also get a very good price on nursery plants if they are in poor condition. The workplace may also be the place to find plants for free that need to be resuscitated. Otherwise, if you are buying, make sure the new growth on a plant is coming in green. If the new growth is yellow, gray, brown, the plant is not a good bet.

FIVE

The Inner Philosophy
of Gardening:
How to Grow a Gardener

*It is the state that counts. Always it is your state that the natural
world responds to, not what you say, not what you do, but what
you are.*

—*The Findhorn Garden*

The inner philosophy of gardening is a subject often over-
looked in our society's obsession with matter rather than
spirit. Ask any gardener what he or she loves about gardening and they will say, "It's how it makes me feel." If
pressed, they say they forget cares and worries, "stop
thinking" and get lost in the process. This deep concentration in Eastern thought is called "becoming one with"
whatever we are doing. It brings deep peace.

Gardening is a natural and refreshing way to enhance
sensitivity to life, to become aware of the mysterious
spiritual transmission that takes place between nature and
humans. With this sensitivity, trees take on a unique per-

sonality, flowers alert you to their essential being, animals and bugs show you their private lives, and birds include you in their play.

In *The Secret Life of Plants*, the authors recount a story about the Indian yogi Ramana Maharshi at his ashram in Southern India. It seems that in the evenings when he went out for his walk, cows from a neighboring village would break from their ropes and run to join him. Local dogs trotted alongside, and young children followed behind. The story goes that even wild animals would emerge from the jungle to accompany him, including various kinds of snakes. Thousands of birds flew low in the sky, hovering over this diverse crew like flying squadrons of protective escorts. When he finished his walk and returned to his room, all his friends disappeared.

Ramana Maharshi had a force field of love that all life gravitated toward instinctively and returned in kind. Growing this kind of love is what spirituality is all about. Every human being has this potential. It is not something that is unattainable. It can become a part of daily life.

The great German poet and literary figure Johann Wolfgang von Goethe fell in love with plants midcareer and devoted himself to watching them grow so he could understand their true essence. He shifted his focus from the literary scene to bringing poetry back into science through his metaphysical understanding of plants.

His first essay on the subject was entitled "On the Metamorphosis of Plants." In it, he brought to bear on the life cycle of a plant the traditional ancient principles of polarity: yin and yang, expansion and contraction, inspiration and expiration, and diastole and systole. For this work Goethe was ignored and ridiculed, rebuked by the scientific community and contemporary society. What he said of the experience was interesting:

> The public demands that every man remain in his own field. Nowhere would anyone grant that science and poetry can be united. People forgot that science had developed from poetry and they failed to take into consideration that a swing of the pendulum might beneficently reunite the two, at a higher level and to mutual advantage.

Many people have moving experiences with trees or while they work in their gardens, but they don't discuss them for fear of sounding silly to relatives and friends. Rarely do people remark on the spiritual aspects of gardening. Instead, gardening often consists of a purely material emphasis, such as adding color to the landscape, accenting the living room with just the right plant, or researching new methods of hybridization and propagation. It is only when someone else broaches the subject of how gardening "feels" that others have the impetus to share their secrets. A personal experience, an epiphany, about the interconnectedness and interdependence of all life as a living reality is a spiritual teaching. It is a gift that marks the beginning of a spiritual perspective, one that incorporates cooperation and communication between plants and humans.

So, the question remains, how does one do it in one's own life? When that question first hit me, twenty years ago, I was citybound and desperate to live in the country. I finally realized I couldn't wait to get "there." I would have to do it "here." I would have to do it now. I needed to begin.

Not everyone has an outdoor garden or lives in the wild. It is a relief to know that the connection can be made anywhere. Take time to make the connection in your own home, even on the smallest scale. Start sensitizing yourself to yourself. Find out who you are. Watch less television. Stay home from the mall. Read and study subjects of interest to you. Talk more deeply to the people who mean something to you. Pay attention to how you feel. Consider those around you and the impact you have on them and your environment.

How can you be sensitive to nature and what is happening in the interplay between you and a tree if you are hardened to your own feelings and those of the people you live and work with every day? If you deny your own inner life, your own inner landscape?

We cover our pain and mask our fear with television, drugs, alcohol, coffee, work, sex, and food. The Zen master Charlotte Joko Beck suggests that our suffering comes from avoiding our real pain. If we allowed ourselves to feel our pain completely in the present moment—by facing it, admitting it, and dealing with it, instead of pushing it away and relegating it to the shadows—we would experience less suffering. Much of the suffering we feel, we add on to our own experience. By refraining from adding self-blame and self-hatred (as well as the other myriad adverse reactions) to the pain, we can change our mental relationship to it. The actual pain itself simply is what it is. It is our negative judgment of it that causes more suffering.

So, you are asking yourself, what does this have to do with relating to nature? We all live here. Making friends with ourselves provides fertile ground for making friends with the world. That means being able to be alone with yourself in the quiet, and listen and feel.

Make time today to slow down. Stop. Be still. Be quiet. Be with yourself and your plants. No experience is required. You can do it either indoors or outdoors. Nature and the plant world will reveal themselves to you in stillness. Your stillness. Your quiet. Your observation. Your concentration. Your aesthetic sense.

Many of us are so used to running, with our bodies and our minds, that we forget nature is happening before our very eyes and within earshot. We just need to slow down to see it and hear it. Even five minutes is worthwhile. Set for yourself an achievable goal and be still with your plants. Be still in your garden. Be still in your heart. Let it unfold. Let nature show herself to you. Then notice how your heart responds. That's it. Very simple. You are a part of it. You are interacting. Nature is noticing you, too.

Once, when I was still living in Manhattan, I met a friend at a sidewalk café on the Upper West Side, near Columbia. We were sitting outside at a table near the only tree on the block. It was a newly planted Gingko that looked naked and vulnerable to the elements, as well as to the roaring traffic zooming by.

About a dozen tiny brown sparrows hopped around on its pathetic branches. Tender green buds were just beginning to open. I remember feeling lucky that there in concrete and traffic, I was having lunch by a tree with birds in it. I remarked to my friend how grateful I was to be near nature, paltry as it might seem in the midst of the city. I pointed to the birds, in particular. She said, "Did it ever occur to you that they are here because of you?"

Of course, it hadn't. But that comment opened my eyes. From that moment on, my perspective of the natural world changed. I became an integral part of life around me. The birds got as much from me as I got from them. And, I wanted to be sure what they got was good.

I began to slow myself down and just sit with my plants, sit with myself. I wanted to be able to think and see and feel and hear better. I became enlivened. Being with myself and my plants in stillness revealed another way of touching and being touched.

Take your growing awareness with you wherever you go. Use it on walks, in other people's homes and gardens, or while you are in the car. You will start noticing things you might have walked by or taken for granted before. Try not to compare your experiences with mine. These stories are only guideposts along the way, possibly corroborating experiences you have already had or alerting you to new possibilities.

Before I started this practice, I was afraid of nature. I had lived in the city so long, anywhere truly wild overwhelmed me. One year, on vacation, my husband and I went to Tobago, a tiny island off the coast of Trinidad. We decided to travel without hotel reservations so we could peruse the island and stay spontaneously wherever we were drawn.

With luck, we discovered a beautiful beach at the far tip of the island, where they rented cottages right on the sand. Being on the lower portion of an old coconut plantation, we could see the owner's house poised high above our bungalow, sheltered mysteriously within a lush over-growth of tropical palms, shrubs, flowers, and vines. One evening, toward the end of our stay, the British owners in-vited us up for a visit. Taking out a worn leather guest book for us to sign, he asked me directly if I felt comfort-able here in the wild. He definitely struck a chord. I smiled and lied that I did, thank you.

In fact, during our entire stay, as darkness descended, I became nervous upon hearing the animals and bugs talking to each other and the wind rustling eerily through the palm trees. Unused to the natural stirring of life teeming within a tropical paradise, I stayed awake nights holding my breath. Too much city asphalt and suburban tract liv-ing and not enough exposure to greenery and growing gar-dens, and what do you get? Disconnection from the earth, from the planet, from others, and from yourself. Far-fetched you say? But it's true. From my perspective, nature had an ominous quality. I sensed its wildness and felt fear.

Maybe that is why we, as postindustrial exiles from na-ture, like to control it. We want everything neat and clean, perfect and tidy. Picture AstroTurf, fake plants, and the unnecessary destruction of mature trees, shrubs, and vines to make way for how *we* want it to look.

A live garden can't look perfect for long if it's allowed to be a natural, growing entity. A garden is a theater in which we can observe plants in the various stages of their life cycle. There's a Zen teaching parable that illustrates the idea that perfection in a garden may not be what we think it is.

Apparently, one of the Zen master's new students had the job of taking care of the garden. One day the Master came out to find that the garden had been severely pruned, immaculately swept, every brown and yellow leaf picked away, and any flower beyond its peak cut off. Instead of being pleased, the teacher moved gently and silently around the garden, delicately spreading a few leaves here and there to give it a windswept look. He said that this was the way to make the garden look perfect, touched by nature's hand rather than overly manipulated by a human one.

People tell me all the time that someone has given them a plant as a gift, or they bought one at the nursery, and it's dying. I've seen enough "dying" plants by now to know that many people's mistaken view of "dying" is actually a natural part of the life cycle. Lower leaves turn brown and die to balance the greening of new growth at the top. I point out that the new growth is green. Yet, because of lack of exposure to the natural processes of life in nature, they have jumped to the conclusion that the plant is dying because it isn't "perfect."

We have come to depend on glossy magazine layouts to give us a yardstick by which to judge nature. Since I began to shift my perspective from the sterile perfection of glamorous magazine photo shoots to the reality of my own garden situation, life has become richer—and simpler. After all, a weed is simply a plant that is growing where you don't want it.

How manicured you keep your garden is surely a matter of taste. I, myself, enjoy a little disarray. It feels more natural and soothing to me to see some flowers on the wane, while others are on the rise. Indoors, I like to keep my plants well groomed. Instead of comparing my garden to an artificial image of how a garden is supposed to look, I stay present with my plants.

The concept of being present, simply being with whatever one is doing, is the quickest and surest way into the natural world. If your mind is elsewhere, preoccupied with the next thing on your agenda, you will miss subtle things.

Once I went to my friend Joan's house. Her husband, Larry, had planted prize sweet peas. Everyone agreed they were the biggest, best, and sweetest-smelling sweet peas they had ever seen. They lasted a few months and then, while they were on the wane, they lost their original vitality and scent.

The sweet peas had climbed their deck and had completely covered one side of the wooden fence. It was hard to believe one package of sweet peas could go so far. I absentmindedly touched a few of the flowers, observing they had lost their delicious fragrance. I called out to Joan, inside the house, "Hey, Joan, the sweet peas don't smell anymore."

Later in the afternoon, after visiting with Joan for a while, I went into the kitchen and was suddenly overwhelmed by the strong scent of sweet peas. I wheeled around and stared out the doorway to the deck, feeling the insistent presence of the flowers. They pitched me a whiff that almost knocked me down.

Their attitude proclaimed, "So there, Miss Handelsman. You thought we didn't smell anymore. Smarty pants. We showed you. We still have it in us."

I find that many people have stories to recount that persuade them of the possibility of communication with their plants or trees. Now that I am in a position to hear these stories at my workshops and lectures, I can vouch for the frequency of their occurrence in the population and the power of their meaning for the people who tell them.

My cousin Mimi told me that after her husband, George, died a wonderful thing happened. George had been an avid gardener. They both enjoyed their time in the garden more than anything they did. They gave Larry, one of George's oldest friends, a gardenia plant from their own greenhouse as a gift. This plant had always bloomed for them.

For three years, Larry couldn't get this gardenia to bloom. He lived in Florida, where gardenias usually bloom twice a year. He did all the right things for it and even had a weekly gardener who fertilized it as part of his garden regimen, but to no avail.

When George died, Mimi called Larry in Florida a few days later to give him the news. Larry said the gardenia had bloomed for the first time the day before. When he heard George died, he was convinced George was saying good-bye to him through the plant.

Indigenous peoples around the world who are in touch

with their native traditions know how to feel this kin-
ship with the natural world. They live this truth daily. It is
as integral to their lives as food, shelter, sex, religion, healing, and well-being. In ancient times, most people were
more easily in touch with their connection to all sentient
beings. We've lost contact with this knowledge in modern
society. For many people, it takes a trip to the wilderness
or a Sunday jaunt to a botanical garden to put them in
touch with that connection once again. The point is, you
do not necessarily have to *go* anywhere. You can create
this feeling wherever you are.

Seventeenth-century Japanese Zen poet Basho gave this
advice to his disciples: "Go to the pine if you want to learn
about the pine, or to the bamboo if you want to learn about
the bamboo. And in doing so, you must let go of your sub-
jective preoccupation with yourself. Otherwise you impose
yourself on the object and don't learn. Your poetry arises by
itself when you and the object have become one, when you
have plunged deep enough into the object to see something like a hidden light glimmering there."

So, if you want to delve more deeply into plants, practice concentrating on them, even for just a few moments.
Practice non-doing. How do you feel when you sit quietly
with them? How do they put out new growth? Under what
circumstances do they bloom? What external stimuli do
they positively or negatively respond to? How are they re-
sponding to your care? Start asking yourself these types of
questions so you can better understand your plants' behavior. Ask the plant to help you. If you do this sincerely, you
will be surprised at the results.

I met a woman who had been sharing her house with a roommate for six years. They purchased houseplants together, but the plants never did well and the flowering plants never bloomed. This woman told me she could never understand why. She took care of them properly, giving them the appropriate light, food, soil, and water. She liked them. But they always seemed droopy and stagnant.

Then after six years the roommate moved out, and immediately all the flowering plants bloomed and the houseplants started to grow significantly. She realized that the plants didn't like the roommate. There had been an external stimulus the plants responded to negatively.

Observe your plants, quietly pay attention to them, feel them. Allow contact to occur. It will start with little things, minute details. You will notice these miracles in quiet moments, in stillness. They will take you by surprise. When it happens, don't push it away by telling yourself it is silly or that the plants cannot understand. The idea is to relate to all living things as if they can understand . . . because they can. Acknowledge this truth. It becomes a reality if you allow it to be so.

The Garden in Venice
and Living My Ideals

Watching gardeners label their plants
   I vow with all beings
to practice the old horticulture
and let plants identify me.

—Robert Aiken Roshi in *The Dragon Who Never Sleeps*,
                    verses for Zen Buddhist practice

"I had a farm in Africa, at the foot of the Ngong Hills." So opens Isak Dinesen's now-famous book *Out of Africa*, her own story of how she married Baron Blixen and lived in Kenya, falling in love with Africa and its people. The book made a profound impression on me as did the movie. I strongly identified with Karen Blixen and her process of transformation from an uppity spoiled brat into an independent, loving, and courageous woman. I wanted that change within myself.

When I first heard Meryl Streep's Danish accent intone

those haunting words, I remembered that once I had felt that way about a place. It wasn't as grand as her coffee plantation in Kenya, but I loved it just the same. I had a farm in Venice, California, at the foot of the Santa Monica Hills.

Actually, my "farm" was a house with a garden, on a well-traveled alley overlooking the Pacific Ocean. It had the distinction of being the first house in Venice, just over the Santa Monica–Venice border. Situated high on a hill in an urban beach town with an Italian namesake, at that moment in my life it was my idea of heaven.

I rented the top floor of a two-story thirties gem. It boasted polished hardwood floors, arched stucco passageways, and a room lined on two adjoining sides with wall-to-wall windows looking out to the sea. Right off the kitchen, out the back porch, a dilapidated, yet well-thought-out, garden lay in shambles at the foot of the stairs.

A retired policeman had planted it when he occupied the place. He had died ten years before and it was clear no one had loved this garden since. Yet, this triangular patch of green, measuring roughly seven hundred square feet, qualified as the only clump of nature in sight.

A knobby old oleander tree grew in the center of it, surrounded by a lawn in sorry shape. A concrete carpet of Bermuda grass, a choking and unrelenting weed, covered a strip alongside the alley planted with rosebushes. I counted twenty-one rosebushes stunted and gasping amidst the mess. Various shrubs and vines grew next to the back of the house including an ancient blue hydrangea in dire need of cutting back and a purple wisteria that wrapped itself around the porch.

On the fence that bordered the adjacent property there lived two huge shade-giving apricot trees with a stand of white Cala lilies underneath. In the evenings, an over-grown Nightqueen shrub filled the air with a sticky, sweet scent I recognized from my travels in India.

A separate garage was almost hidden by gobs of orange lantana running rampant across its roof. Even though this vining shrub was out of control, the posylike flowers lent a cheerful accent to the ramshackle nature of the garden.

A broken-down picket fence, which may have once pro-tected the plot from cars, people, cats, and dogs, had been smashed into so many times by neighbors and tourists parking where they shouldn't have that it was barely func-tional. When I moved in, the garden was a refuse dump for lazy locals on their way to the beach.

My attitude was one of judgment. As far as I was con-cerned, everyone who disrespected the garden needed re-forming, and I presumed to be the one to convert them. Without even being conscious of it, I had a pious mission-ary and a sanctimonious zealot closeted in my psyche. I didn't know yet that I was the one who needed conversion.

Two years had passed since my divorce. I had recently moved to California from Manhattan, and I believed I was lucky to have a plot of green that looked to me like a tiny piece of country plunked down amid the asphalt. By the appearance of the place, no one could call it a dream house in the woods, but the apartment was spacious and sunny and renting it gave me my first chance to play outdoors in a garden.

I worried that I didn't know what I was doing and that I

needed experts to help me revitalize the plot. However, I wanted a vegetable garden more than I wanted to indulge my fear and nagging self-doubt, so I resolved to plant something wonderful. I'd simply learn on the job. I summoned up my latent moxie and went to work.

Maybe I could bring back the roses, I mused. That meant digging up the formidable amount of hardcore Bermuda grass. "You'll never do it," native Californians cried. "The roots are impossible to extract." I decided not to listen to them. Never listen to negative gardening advice. You don't know what is possible until you try.

My boyfriend, Bob, had just moved in with me, so I enlisted his aid to start digging. He was skeptical and had to be coaxed, exhorted, and finally begged to help me. The physical labor was beyond any expectation of "difficult" we had imagined. The Bermuda grass certainly lived up to its cranky reputation. As Bob pointed out so cogently, when he was sweaty and whipped by the work, "These roots stretch to China!"

But we kept at it for a week, becoming obsessed with it, compulsively ripping out every last smidgen. At this point in my education as a gardener, it didn't occur to me to give notice to the smothering Bermuda grass. I just wanted to get rid of it. Interspersed with the weeds were caseloads of nasty rocks that also had to be sifted out of the soil and removed. When we were done, the feeling of accomplishment was fantastic. I stood on the newly turned plot, grabbing the hoe in my hand as if I had just reached the top of Mt. Everest and was claiming it for my country. I was beginning to feel like a bona fide outdoor gardener.

"At last," I exclaimed, "the roses can breathe again." We dug deep wells around each bush to hold the extra water they craved and added some homemade horse manure tea to feed them. I looked forward to watering time with great anticipation, when I would scan the roses for new growth and urge them to bud.

It was quite a moment when all the roses bloomed. By midsummer, we were cutting bouquets for the house, choosing from twenty-one varieties. There were the classic red ones (Abe Lincolns), yellow, orange, orange-red (which smelled the best), silver (which reminded me of funerals), and pure white. I was beside myself with happiness.

The *pièce de résistance* was the kitchen garden. There was plenty of space to put in vegetables and herbs. I read Rudolph Steiner, the Austrian philosopher and educator who started the Anthroposophical Society in 1923. He touted a philosophy that embraced a spiritual view of the human being, asserting that humanity (*anthropos*) has the inherent wisdom (*sophia*) to transform both itself and the world. Steiner taught a series of lectures called "The Agriculture Course," in which he outlined Biodynamic Gardening, a method of intensive soil preparation and organic planting that employs planetary influences, cosmic rhythms, and sensitive observation to grow a healthy and abundant garden.

I particularly liked that he said to put all of yourself, including your thoughts and your determination, into what you do in your garden. He believed everything in the physical world is suffused and molded by your will and your spirit, so what comes out of the soil is a reflection of what you have put into it of yourself. I had yet to realize that this theory also works in reverse. The garden would grow me.

I took an adult gardening course at the local Waldorf School, where they educate children according to Steiner's theories. My teacher combined Biodynamics with French Intensive gardening, employing an arduous method of preparing beds called double-digging. An integral part of the gardening class consisted of a hands-on experience every weekend at each one of the classmates' homes when we all pitched in to double-dig their beds.

Double-digging intensive beds loosens and aerates the soil twenty-four inches down. These beds create a growing medium that enables the plant roots to easily penetrate the soil and receive a consistent supply of organic nourishment.

The weekend we came to my house, we dug four long, narrow beds of varying sizes using this elaborate method. First we spread compost, horse and steer manure, cotton-seed meal, bone meal and live oak leaf mulch over the ap-pointed area. We dug a trench one foot deep and one foot wide across the width of each rectangular bed, moving the displaced soil to the other end of the bed. Then we loos-ened the next foot down in the trench with a spading fork to break up clumps and compaction. We proceeded to the next square foot trench, carefully moving each spadeful of dirt forward, mixing the soil layers as little as possible. When we completed our task, the initial square foot of soil was used to fill the last trench at the other end.

By the end of the day everyone was exhausted, but the teacher said this initial stage demanded the most work. Digging the beds was certainly labor-intensive, he conceded; however, future maintenance and weeding would be minimal.

There was so much to learn about the Biodynamic method. I knew it would take time, so I did what I could and ultimately told myself that anything I did was better than nothing. That spring I stopped worrying about doing it right and just did it, period. It was very liberating.

I planted everything we loved to eat: collard greens and mustard; white wax beans and spinach; arugula and three different kinds of lettuce: oak leaf, bronze, and Bibb. We put in a border of nasturtiums so we could add the pungent edible orange flowers to salads and companion planted bushes of sweet basil with the tomatoes to keep us in pesto. Steiner recommended planting seven specific herbs and flowers to enhance the growth of the garden so we made sure we had borage, chamomile, stinging nettle, yarrow, calendula, comfrey, and dandelion.

By the time we harvested our crop, the garden had grown so tall and dense, I had to push back massive amounts of bumper to bumper plants when I walked into the thick of it to pick our food. I had never seen borage grow before. It protected the tomatoes and its tiny purple-blue flowers tasted delicious and looked like shooting stars. The dandelion made a terrific green salad, stinging nettle attracted butterflies, and the soft orange calendula flowers, known medicinally to soothe skin irritations, practically glowed in the dark.

Even though I was gardening according to spiritual methods, my attitude toward the people around me was decidedly base. I thought I was so holy planting the garden yet I hated the people who crashed into the fence, threw beer cans into the tomato patch and flicked burning cigarettes onto the roses. Certainly I was better than they were. I was healing the earth; they were slobs. On the outside I was "nice" but on the inside I was seething. I was trying to create a thing of beauty while the neighbors couldn't have cared less.

To fend off outsiders, I delineated the property line with flowers, vainly hoping for a twenty-foot wall to grow. I lined the sagging fence with tiny cosmos I had planted from seed, determined to cover up the distinct lack of charm. Dutifully, I picked up cigarette butts and fast-food wrappers every day, pacing up and down the length of the alley muttering under my breath in disgust.

Beer bottles abounded, diet soda cans and empty wine jugs appeared on a less regular basis. At least if there had been some beer left in the bottles, I could have used it to catch the snails, I grumbled to myself. Drunken snails are helpless to suck the life out of plants after they've been imbibing beer in a shallow pan all night. It bugged me that I had to buy beer for my snails while I got the bottles and cans for free, courtesy of unthinking passersby.

Every time I planted something new, I could almost guarantee that the next day I'd find a local dog had made its mark right next to it. Besides being incensed at having to clean up other people's dog excrement, it irked me that the roaming dogs would know exactly when to crush a newly planted seedling or a recently sprouted seed.

This negative internal attitude did me no good when my "party animal" neighbors drove by, blaring their car radios and oblivious to the toil going on over the fence. It didn't help me, either, when we manured the vegetable beds and the man across the way complained bitterly because "the place smelled like shit." Didn't he know it was clean shit?

My resentment ate me up inside, and I ranted self-righteously at the dinner table every night. Bob chastened me, saying, "Judy, that man's the Buddha, too, you know." But, at the time, I didn't understand that God lived within my snide and obtuse neighbor, too. Sure, I knew God was in everybody, but only theoretically. How could God be inside *that* body?

I was being brought to my knees. Nothing was changing on the outside. However, I began to get the message that whatever I did, I did for myself and because I wanted to do it. I couldn't expect everyone else to kiss my feet because I thought I was right. I told myself, "You may plant the seeds but *you* don't make them grow. Somebody else does that." I needed to lighten up. So, I went about my business in the yard, wrestling like Jacob with the angel, coming face-to-face with my spiritual arrogance and petty self-righteousness. Instead of looking out, I needed to give myself to the garden.

Underneath the oleander tree, I planted margarita daisies that soon swelled to bush size and encircled the trunk like a sash of flowers. I began to see that in California people took oleander for granted. Noted for its hardiness and imperviousness to exhaust fumes, it is used as a common shrub for massive plantings along the freeways. Our tree, with its heavy barky trunk, looked spectacular when it bloomed a truly innocent pink.

From the bedroom and our office, I could almost touch the tree. I'd look out onto it and get lost in the swirling mass of sensuous blossoms, surveying the garden proudly from a bird's-eye view. I remember that room in which I wrote with great nostalgia. It shimmered like a bejeweled garret in the sparkling blue sky of California ocean light. The omnipresent sea breeze made me feel as if I were on perpetual vacation.

Eager to add plants to our home, I scanned the newspapers often for garage sales. One day I drove to Pacific Palisades for a moving sale featuring garden items. Ironically, the woman was returning to New York and selling everything she had. For forty dollars, I walked away with rare old begonias, unusual bromeliads, and a staghorn fern that resembled giant antlers, the kind you'd see hanging on a wall in an old hunting lodge.

This staghorn fern had a blatant animallike personality. When I got it home, we arranged it outside on the front porch, overlooking the street. After a while, I thought it was lonely out there and didn't look very comfortable. So, during a cold spell in December, Bob and I brought it inside—not an easy task, since it was so big. As we lugged it around a corner of the hallway next to the inside staircase, we lost our grip and the staghorn toppled down the stairs onto its face.

"Oh, my God," I moaned, "we've killed it." I ran down the stairs to pick it up and held it next to me, rocking it, apologizing for being so clumsy, beseeching it to live. Bob soothed me, saying he was certain it would be all right.

"When it warms up a little, we'll hang it in the garden under one of the trees. That's where it belongs," he assured me. So we lived with it in the hallway, spraying it with water once in awhile until the cold spell passed, and then carried it out to the apricot tree when the frost was over. We ceremoniously hung it on a protrusion of the apricot's trunk and wished it well.

To make it feel at home and to celebrate its anthropomorphic presence, I planted some of my favorite annuals underneath it: Johnny-jump-ups, pansies, and Crystal Palace lobelia, a flower that has one of the most remarkable blue-violet colors that exists in the plant kingdom. When it grows in large blocks, the effect is eye-popping. Medicinally, it was listed in my herbal book as an antispasmodic, so I figured that a calming influence emitted from its sheer presence.

I took special pleasure in watering these flowers. I splurged on a device called a wand. When I held it in a certain way, the water made an arc, simulating natural rainfall and gracing the plants with a softer and more delicate shower than the usual hosing.

By the time I moved three years later, the staghorn fern had tripled in size and had wrapped itself around the trunk of the apricot tree in a massive hug. It guarded the elegant calla lilies and the odoriferous Nightqueen and spread its protective wing over the violas and the lobelia. The staghorn received so much attention and affection as the focal point of this shady moist section of the garden, it flourished.

Doris, the long-term tenant downstairs, told me that the two old apricot trees hadn't borne fruit in ten years. I had been so busy loving the flowers underneath them, I hadn't paid much heed to the trees. My neglect became a lesson in the power of indirect love. The apricots reaped the benefits from the attention I gave the flowers.

One day, I looked up into the trees and noticed they had blossoms. When the apricots formed, I was delirious and Doris was incredulous. We picked enough apricots to fill three laundry baskets, and no matter how much jam I made or how many pies I baked, we couldn't eat all the fruit, so we gave away apricots to the neighbors and heaped them on friends.

Giving away food from the garden awakened new feelings in me. A generosity of spirit, a desire to nurture others with nature's bounty and a sense of what it meant to be "Mother Earth" all surfaced within me. Something was changing. Everything I loved about gardening—the messiness, the abandon, the abundance—was happening to my spirit.

One day in March, I noticed tiny green points peeking up through the soil on both sides of the garden path. Walking back and forth from the garage to our back stairs, we diligently followed their progress. Before we knew it, we were knee-deep in narcissus. It was a lavish surprise to be so inundated. We cut bunches and bunches of narcissus, filling every room in the house with their almost cloying sweetness. We gave away armfuls to neighbors and loaded up friends whenever they came to visit.

The garden was uncontainable. Funny, I thought, how they call gardening in pots "container gardening." They should call gardens in the soil "uncontainable gardening." I worked on the garden and it worked on me. I couldn't maintain my rigid world view, my black and white thinking, and still garden. After all, in the garden, a weed is just a weed. It's not good or bad. It's just a plant in a place you don't want it. The awareness didn't happen overnight, but during that time, the seeds were planted within me for work I would do on myself for the rest of my life. As the garden grew, I couldn't stand still.

Once, a friend from San Francisco paid us a call. We sat in that room, the one above the garden that elicited such magic in my own mind, and as he looked out the windows he said, "You think this is beautiful? Don't you think all those telephone poles are ugly?"

I felt physically shocked by his words, as if he had wielded a blow to my chest. I had developed a maternal love for my garden. It felt as if he had just impugned the looks of one of my children. "Sure, my kid has a few pimples on her chin," I thought to myself, "but I don't notice them. Look at her eyes and hair and those long, shapely legs." Like a mother with a child, I had been interacting with a living organism day after day. Didn't he know that that creates love?

For me, what had happened in the garden was like falling in love with a man who, upon first impression, isn't good-looking, but becomes beautiful after his character reveals itself and you see his soul. It wasn't love at first sight between me and the garden, but as I interacted with it, I grew to love it unconditionally.

After that time, I realized that the experience of growing a garden was different than I had thought in the beginning. I was gardening not to create a garden; I was gardening simply to garden. The process yielded the joy; the results were secondary. As Alan Chadwick, himself a master of the Biodynamic/French Intensive method, once said, "The gardener does not make the garden: the garden makes the gardener."

I poured heavy doses of physical and psychic energy into the garden. I was out in the alley every day watering, weeding, digging, and planting. For my birthday, Bob gave me a statue of St. Fiacre, the patron saint of gardens and gardeners. Dressed in a cowled robe with a rosary hanging from his braided belt, he had a meditative air about him. He held a shovel in one hand and a book in the other and silently blessed the garden from his niche in the oleander tree.

I looked up his name in an old herbal book and learned that during the Middle Ages, St. Fiacre gave up the worldly life as a prince of Ireland to live as a monk in a hermitage situated on the edge of a forest near Meaux, France. So many people came to him for healing that he began cultivating herbs and flowers to aid those in need. His reputation as both a gardener and a healer spread.

He built his own monastery at Breuil, where he continued to nurture his beloved plants as well as the people who flocked to see him. His little statue was my inspiration-in-residence, attesting to the importance of putting love into the neighborhood as well as into the garden. I was learning in a humbling way that I couldn't pour love into my garden and stop it at the front gate. My love had to overflow. I was going to have to coexist with the dogs and the cats, the neighbors and the tourists, without trying to change them. All I could do was work on myself.

By summer, the garden started to pop. The lettuces headed, the tomato plants hung heavy with fat juicy beef-steaks, and the nasturtiums gushed with brilliant color. The neighbors began to notice something different next door. They leaned over the fence, now camouflaged by the cosmos, and started to ask questions about what was what. I enjoyed talking to anyone who showed an interest and handed them a head of lettuce or a fistful of flowers when they went on their way.

Neighbors who had never met before engaged each other in conversation. Frank, the man in the apartment complex across the alley who used to complain about the smell of the garden, said now it made him feel good and that it hadn't looked this nice since John, the retired cop, lived there. It turned out that Frank, the man I had previously written off as snide and godless, liked flowers, so I gave him a bouquet. As for the fence, it wasn't so easy to crash into anymore now that such beauty beamed out from its boundaries. Word about the garden spread throughout the neighborhood. Soon, other gardening aficionados came by with cuttings and to swap plant stories. Tourists stopped and perused the place on their way to the beach. The garden became an oasis of friendliness, an excuse to talk with people, a chance to stop in a busy day and shoot the breeze. Gardeners love to talk about gardening, and I was available to gab.

What I had wanted to achieve, then had relinquished as

a goal, happened anyway. The garden humanized the community, and that included me. It gave us a spiritual center, a reason to connect and interact. It became a "town square." It also became clear that I had to be fanatically careful not to become a fanatic.

In my heart, I moved to the country that summer. I indulged my farm-girl fantasies, reveling in dirt and mud and water and feeling close to the earth in the midst of a city. Farm girls know their neighbors, and I got to know mine. By the end of the summer, we had a sense of community.

I lived to be in that garden. I became so connected to it that one night I had a dream. I was looking out my bedroom window, onto the double-dug beds, and saw a tiny cosmos rise up out of the soil. I watched it grow, as in time-lapse photography, from a tiny seedling to a blooming flower. I knew that flower was me and I was watching myself grow. When I awoke, I told Bob my dream. I asked him if he thought I was psychotic. He just said, "You're the Buddha, too, Judy."

Biodynamic Gardening and the French Intensive Method

Practical activity nowadays is an empty routine devoid of spirit; but anything that truly does come from the spirit is always preeminently practical.

—Rudolf Steiner, 1924

Already in 1924 in Germany, Rudolf Steiner was asking the kind of questions that have become more and more common here in the United States. In his series of lectures called *Agriculture*, he posited, "Why, for instance, is it no longer possible to find potatoes as good as the ones I ate when I was a boy? . . . Potatoes like those are simply not found anymore, not even in the places where I used to eat them." Steiner's biodynamics focuses on farming and agriculture, but it is also applicable to all types of gardening. Biodynamics at its core is the marriage of science to a spiritual worldview he called Anthroposophy.

Steiner described his ideology as "awareness of one's humanity." Anthroposophy looks at human potential as the source of hope and regeneration that can lead us out of planetary crisis. It is through human consciousness that we can heal our relationship to the earth and to each other.

Biodynamic agriculture is one aspect of Anthroposophy in action. It draws a direct connection between the quality of food, human health, and human awareness. Rather than a static body of knowledge and a presentation of practical techniques, Biodynamics is a lifelong study of human interrelationship with nature through precise observation, clear thinking, and spiritual insight. There are basic tenets and instruction, but the path is infinite and open at all times to new and miraculous individual discovery precisely because it depends not on dogma but on human interaction.

Biodynamics involves a complete restoration of the soil, the foundational element necessary to yield high-quality food rich in nutritional value, vitality, and good, sweet taste. The earth (soil) and the plants are in a symbiotic relationship. The roots of a plant reach down into the earth for the minerals to sustain and nourish. Through water, the roots take in minerals from a healthy, well-balanced soil and feed the plant. The connection between the plant and the soil is vital. By feeding plants soluble chemical fertilizer, we have detoured this relationship. Essentially our food is disconnected from its true source. The plants are no longer feeding off Mother Earth, but instead being artificially boosted. The soil has simply become a medium for chemically prepared liquid nutrients. No matter what kind of gardening we do, the plants and the earth need each other both physically and spiritually. Think about it. If you cut off the connection between a parent and a child, there is an emotional deprivation that occurs. Symbolically, the same can be said of the food we eat and the way we grow it. How can we expect food to taste good and nourish us properly if it has lost its rightful connection to its source?

Chemical fertilizers kill earthworms and deaden the soil. Soil should be alive, a living system, loaded with beneficial microorganisms that help plants use the nitrogen from the air, and fat, juicy earthworms that provide castings rich in nutriments. Building a well-balanced soil through correct composting is the goal. Incorporated in this philosophy, Steiner insisted that we must put our spirit, our mind, our heart and soul, into a garden. We can do this consciously through our efforts and our intention. What we get back will be a reflection of what we have put in of ourselves.

Steiner taught that by including the cosmos as a direct influence upon what happens on the planet Earth, we can have a balanced garden. He pointed out that all living things are interrelated, so we cannot garden in a vacuum, focusing purely on what is occurring with one plant or one pest. Everything is connected. Aptly stated, Steiner explains:

> I have said many times that if you have a compass needle, which always points in the same direction— one end toward magnetic north, the other end toward magnetic south—people would find it childish if you said the reason for this lay in the needle itself. They would tell you that it is . . . Earth's magnetic north pole and south pole that determine the needle's alignment. You have to look away from the needle itself and take into account the entire Earth in order to explain how the needle behaves. People will think you are quite childish if you believe that what you see in a plant depends on what science discovers in the immediate surroundings of that plant. In fact, the whole starry heaven is involved in the growth of plants.

So the basis of Biodynamics is an attitude shift from compartmentalizing plants and seeing them out of context from the environment to expanding our view of them to include all the forces of nature such as the light of the sun, the movements of the moon as it passes through the constellations, the position of the planets, the rotation of the earth on its axis as it makes a complete revolution each day, as well as the deep currents of life within the earth itself.

According to Biodynamics, the four elements—earth, water, air, and fire, respectively—influence the development of the roots, leaves, flowers, and fruit-seed. These elements are reflected in the twelve signs of the zodiac. The earth signs are Taurus, Virgo, and Capricorn. The water signs are Cancer, Scorpio, and Pisces. The air signs are Gemini, Libra, and Aquarius. The fire signs are Aries, Leo, and Sagittarius. The moon is the conduit through which the earth receives the elemental forces of the constellations as it passes through each sign during its twenty-eight-day cycle.

The earth element affects the growth of the roots. This is easy to see, simply by the fact that the roots penetrate the soil. The water element, through the phases of the moon and its gravitational pull, influences the development of the leaves. This can be seen by the water retained in vegetables. As soon as they are cooked or pressed, water is released. The water accounts for juiciness. When watering a garden appropriately, watch what happens. The plants perk up considerably after watering, becoming bouncy and turgid, full of water. The air element influences the development of flowers as they open out into it. Fire influences the development of fruit-seed. The warmth of the sun contributes to the ripening of fruit and the maturing of seeds.

Although this may seem far-fetched to some, Steiner's followers have conducted extensive scientific experiments to prove the efficacy of their theories.

Maria Thun, a German farmer, has done the most no-
table research in the field for the last forty years. Spon-
sored for ten years by the West German government to
carry out observations and tests on an experimental
farm, Thun publishes a yearly agricultural calendar that
makes the data tracing these cosmic rhythms available
to farmers and gardeners around the world through the
efforts of the Biodynamic network.

Central to Biodynamic farming and gardening are
what its proponents call the Biodynamic preparations.
These combinations are prepared from chamomile,
yarrow, dandelion, oak bark, and stinging nettle. They
are used at certain times of the year, directly on the
earth to stimulate the life in the soil, in the compost
pile, and on the leaves of plants to encourage their intake of light.

Biodynamics is a rich scientific and philosophical
discipline that people spend their lives studying. They
live it within themselves and in their farms and gardens.
It is impossible to give a comprehensive overview of it
in the scope of this book and do it justice. But, through
reading, and particularly through doing, the concepts
grow on you, so to speak, and take on a life of their
own. The spiritual philosophy sets it apart from other
gardening methods. At whatever level you may choose
to pursue the principles, it will broaden your percep-
tions to deeper levels of relationship to the plants and
the wonders of gardening.

A garden teaches in the most basic and elemental
way. It broadcasts a silent but articulate curriculum that
is easy to understand simply by showing up and paying
attention. Alan Chadwick was a man who knew this in

every cell of his body. An Englishman who drew a great deal on Rudolf Steiner, Chadwick brought together Biodynamic gardening with the French Intensive method when he was invited by the University of California at Santa Cruz to teach in the 1960s. The student garden he developed on four acres of land grew out of a hillside with poor clayey soil. The only thing that grew there was poison oak. In two to three years, without the use of machines, Chadwick and his students returned the barren soil to a high level of fertility, growing beautiful and fragrant flowers and tasty healthy vegetables in yields four times greater than those produced by commercial agriculture.

Chadwick was an artist and a formally trained English actor. He showed students how a garden can be an artistic and creative endeavor, nourish a meditative inner life, and bring the soul closer to its primal connection to the earth through building a living soil. He taught the combination of two agricultural movements started in Europe. One was Biodynamics and the other, French Intensive gardening, developed outside Paris in the late 1800s. There, they grew plants in eighteen inches of manure. Planted closely together in such an intensive space, the foliage touched and provided a canopy of living mulch that kept down the weeds and kept the moisture in. The growing medium was so rich and friable, the practitioners of the French Intensive method grew many crops a year with high yields. During the winter, large glass bell jars were placed over plants such as lettuce, to keep them warm and to protect the new seedlings from frost. They even grew melons during the coldest months of the year.

Both Biodynamics and the French Intensive method share similar gardening procedures such as raised beds, companion planting (pairing plants that encourage each other's growth and health), and crop rotation. In his book *How to Grow More Vegetables Than You Ever Thought Possible on Less Land Than You Can Imagine*, John Jeavons (of Ecology Action) brings together these two methods to make this type of gardening accessible to everyone. He, too, was influenced by Chadwick and continues to work to encourage community-based farming and gardening in Willits, California.

SEVEN

Late Bloomer and the
Praying Mantises

How little we know as yet of the life of plants—their hopes and fears, pains and enjoyments!

—John Muir, *A Thousand Mile Walk to the Gulf*, 1916

I am a late bloomer. The standard garden variety. My mother always told me this and I began to believe her as I reached my early forties and was still in the process of trying to figure it all out. But, you know how you know things and then *you know them?* This is what happened to me through the process of watching my garden.

For the sake of my story, I want to bring you up-to-date on my long-term relationship with cosmos. I have built a strong foundation with them over the years. I even plant them at friends' houses because I love them so much. I usually grow an extra flat and then take the seedlings to people I know will appreciate them. If there is a patch of dirt or a couple of big pots that are empty, in go a few cosmos.

The first time I ever saw cosmos was about eighteen years ago, at the house of friends in Cornwall, Connecticut. Being a city girl, I hardly knew anything back then about flowers, let alone how to grow them. The extent of my appreciation was going downstairs to the florist on the corner of 108th Street and Broadway in Manhattan and picking out the prettiest and freshest ones the owner had in the refrigerator. I would learn all the names of the flowers by asking what they were called and how much they cost. I was flabbergasted when I finally moved to Santa Monica and could actually pick Birds of Paradise on the street outside the food co-op where I shopped. I kept telling everyone, "These cost $7.50 apiece in New York!"

The barn siding in Cornwall was gray and weathered. Everything not only looked old, it *was* old. About a half dozen of the white-petaled variety of cosmos were planted, bumper-to-bumper, in front of an antique artifact placed strategically on the lawn. I don't remember anymore what it was, perhaps an old carriage wheel or piece of farm equipment. The effect was eye-catching. I did a double-take.

The white flowers had golden yellow centers dotted with black. Their foliage was feathery and graceful. They were a cliché, for heaven's sake, swaying in the breeze creating a perfect foil for that museum piece. Later, I discovered cosmos also came in pink and magenta. There are true orange ones, too, whose configuration is much smaller. To my chagrin these days, I am only able to find seed packets with mixed colors. This year I am saving seed from the white ones only, in what may be the vain hope I can recreate my friend's rustically elegant display.

The first year I ever planted cosmos, I had the garden in Venice. I planted three flats of cosmos and then transplanted the tiny seedlings adjacent to the fence. To my great surprise and delight, they came up. And they were huge! They filled in so densely that they created a four-foot hedge, convincing me of their beauty and dependability. I manicured them well, carefully snipping off the dead heads so the new buds would blossom, and I trimmed them often for bouquets.

The cosmos grew to be picture-postcard perfect. Cosmos are one of those flowers that, no matter where you plant them in profusion, they achieve that photogenic quality. They grow practically everywhere, from lush gardens to slivers of dust on the sides of asphalt. Their seeds spread easily and volunteer year after year. Even in poor soil, they hardly ever look bad.

When I moved away from Venice, and many years later, into a "mother-in-law's" apartment in the eastern Sierra of California, the people who rented to me gave me a small plot at the edge of their garden. From it I could see the snow-capped mountains of the Sierra range. Their peaks glistened all winter in the clear mountain light, and I never tired of how the light played off of them.

A weathered redwood fence surrounded the plot on three sides. I planted a mixed color packet of cosmos seeds along two sides of the fence to punctuate my double-dug bed of Japanese eggplants, sweet basil, curly parsley, and sweet 100 tomatoes.

As part of my effort to provide a meaningful, personal touch to the environment, I hung a prayer flag made out of gauze imprinted with a green medieval woodcut depicting the sun and the moon hanging in the sky, suspended like caricatures over a garden path winding into infinity.

I figured I needed both the sun and the moon, the masculine and the feminine, the creative and the receptive, the yin and the yang, to help this garden grow. So I decided these archetypes were appropriate images to hang on the fence. When the wind blew, the vibratory meaning of the symbols would spread throughout the garden in the same manner that they did in the mountain monasteries of Tibet, where they hung prayer flags with Tibetan mantras inscribed on them. It couldn't hurt, I thought.

During this time, I taught art history at the local community college. For her term project, a student gave me a rock she had painted to look like an ancient petroglyph. I placed it on the fence near the prayer flag, along with an old horseshoe someone had given me for good luck. These icons were my substituted version of other ritual garden statues I had known and loved before, such as St. Fiacre and St. Francis of Assisi.

I planted my trusted cosmos in mid-May. By the end of June they were profuse. By August they were higher than the fence and radiated that postcard effect that I so much admired. The white ones were particularly showy. Crisp, clean, and simple.

I would cut a mixed bouquet every few days for the house. When I first got the cosmos inside, they would droop. Then, within a few minutes of being in water, they would perk up in their vase and gracefully project the epitome of unified chaos.

By July I noticed there was one cosmos plant that was huge but had no buds. There was plenty of foliage but not one bud. In spite of myself, I had negative thoughts whenever I looked at it. I viewed it with disdain and thought to myself, "What a dud," or "Maybe, I'll dig you out and throw you away. You aren't doing anything!" It's hard for me to believe I thought those things in view of what transpired.

I just kept on silently bad-mouthing that one cosmos plant whenever I saw it. The others were models of expected behavior. They grew to be almost as tall as I and were randomly dotted with flowers and buds. The more I picked, the more they bloomed, a truism in the world of flowers.

Still, I wanted to get rid of the one that wasn't blooming. As I look back, I was full of doubt and gave it no encouragement. In fact, I mentally beat it down. I wanted to pull it out because it wasn't fitting into my idea of how the garden *should* be. There was a part of me that was saying, "If it doesn't do what I want, I'll just kill it."

Despite my negativity, something kept telling me to stop thinking in that way and let the cosmos plant just be. Maintaining this negative attitude certainly didn't fit into my garden credo. So time passed, and for a while I forgot about the plant, assuming it would always stay the way it was. I gave it no credit for growing at its own pace and in its own fashion. "Something major is wrong with it," I arrogantly decided. I figured it had just forgotten about blooming, particularly because it was already as tall and as full as the others and they were already full of flowers.

Then, one hot day in September, after ignoring the cosmos for a long time, I absentmindedly looked at it again. I was taken aback at what I saw. The entire cosmos plant was filled with buds. Within two weeks that plant was heavily laden with giant blooms. All of the other cosmos along the fence were on the wane by now.

The one I had demeaned was fuller than any of the others. If I stood on my tiptoes and stretched out my arms as far as I could, in either direction, it was still taller and wider than I. Its stem was as thick as the circle I made when I touched my thumbs and forefingers of both hands together around it.

I remembered my harsh judgments as the summer had progressed. All this time I had felt superior to the cosmos plant. In fact, we were *both* late bloomers. It was reminding me how late bloomers feel because some people (including themselves) think they aren't as big or strong or productive or beautiful as they "should" be. Then, in the end, when they bloom, they go beyond all comparisons. Late bloomers may take longer to develop and may look as if they will never amount to much, but, when they do bloom, they are special. They may even have *more* to offer.

This late bloomer grew taller, wider, thicker, and more profusely than any of the other cosmos along the fence. In fact, I've never seen one that big and I am a cosmos aficionado. They call out to me, even when they are hidden on hillsides, nestled in neighbors' backyards, or sticking up as volunteers between the concrete slabs on the street.

As a final tribute to the cosmos, three big-bellied pregnant praying mantises took up residence in its foliage. I
would visit them every day and talk to them. They had
that "E.T." look as they twisted their heads on those long,
ringed necks, tilting them up at me and staring with
bulging glass eyes. I blew them kisses and billed and cooed
as if they were my babies. Their antennae would shift back
and forth when I talked. If I brought other people to see
them, they would hide. They were there just for me.

The mantises nested in the most significant plant in my
garden, the one I had snickered at and castigated for fail-
ing to live up to my expectations. Now that plant was
hostess to the mystical praying mantises. It was as if the
cosmos were being sanctioned by these friendly beings,
metaphorically crowned for its efforts to bloom.

The dictionary says that the root of *mantis* is Greek for
prophet or seer. The root of *cosmos* is Greek for harmony
and universe. What a pair, I mused, as I pondered the high
roots that gripped my garden and admired how it all fit together so meaningfully.

By October, the cosmos was dying off and becoming
brittle. The foliage turned brown and the dead flower
heads dried out, so I was able to collect seed for the following year. One morning, as I made my daily trek to the
back of the garden plot, I saw that the late bloomer had
keeled over. The stem had broken off at its base. I lifted it
gently, moaning as I did, wondering if the mantises had
flown. I used a brick to prop up the plant, hoping I could
preserve the mantis home intact.

At first it was hard to find them. I searched the entire

bush. Suddenly, when I was ready to give up, there they were. Vaguely pink and chameleonlike on the dying plant, they were very still. It was then I knew our time together was almost up.

They had been my friends. They had magically let me get to know them. I would miss them and the late-blooming cosmos. Because of them, I had hope I wouldn't judge myself as harshly as I usually did, and learn to trust and respect my own time to bloom.

When I went to the garden the next day, the prophets and seers were gone. The following spring, while I was planting tomatoes, I found an empty praying mantis egg case on one of the circular tomato stakes. I took note of it and continued planting.

In the Bishop garden, I experimented with the Ruth Stout method of gardening. She advocated laying down single sheets of newspaper over prepared soil, eventually building the layers to three or four sheets. Then she advised watering the layers of paper thoroughly and poking holes in them to plant seeds and seedlings.

The wet paper should then be covered with straw and watered. The straw sinks, transforming itself into an aromatic carpet of mulch to keep weeds down and moisture in. Since I was living in the high desert, water conservation was an issue of the highest priority.

As with double-digging, the first steps were a lot of work, but after that weeds were minimal and the watering manageable. The day I finally finished all the planting, I relaxed in my usual fashion by watering the garden. In my view, watering after a day of planting is the ultimate pleasure. Everything washes clean in a matter of moments, and the garden shines with a fresh new identity.

I was patting myself on the back, surveying my kingdom, when I spied a neon-green spot standing out in bas relief on the wet fence. I squinted and moved closer, pointing the hose in the opposite direction. I peered at the green squiggle and, sure enough, inching up the wall was a baby praying mantis, the first of the season. I could have thought, "Ah, that's just a coincidence." Instead I chose to feel welcomed back to my garden by my friends, the praying mantises.

"Full circle," I smiled.

P.S. As I finished writing this book, the first batch of my white cosmos bloomed. I picked a bouquet and placed it on my desk. As their black and white and yellow faces stared up at me from their home in the vase, I remembered back to this story, the first chapter I ever wrote, seven years before. I would call that perfect timing, wouldn't you?

On Watering

> The highest good is like water. Water gives life to the ten thousand things and does not strive. It flows in places men reject and so is like the Tao.
>
> —Lao-Tzu, *Tao-te Ching*

What to say about the curative power of hoses on such cumbersome maladies as impatience, frustration, and anger? Dealing with the curse, or should I say challenge, of the hose is a lesson in equipoise. I can't say that I have mastered this feat even after twenty years of gardening practice. As a matter of fact, I have come to believe that the hose exists to try our characters. It tempers our distemper with humility and reminds us, I can't resist saying it, of the importance of going with the flow.

One of the most instructive lessons inherent in gardening is its quality of fluidity. Whether the garden lives in containers or grows in the ground, a garden is never done, never finished. There is no resolution. It is an ongoing organic entity. Just when you think you've got it how you want it, something needs repotting or transplanting and change has to occur. Just when you think it's perfect, you bring in something new and there's movement again. Even as a garden lies dormant in the winter, it is gathering power in the underworld to rise forth again in the spring. Persephone must serve her six months underground.

In the life cycle of a plant, we can see the interplay of past, present, and future. A look at gardening with this perspective teaches the constancy of change and offers a fulcrum around which we can maintain our equilibrium through life's transitions. The *I Ching* or *Book of Changes*, the ancient Chinese system of divination in which Taoism and Confucianism have their common roots, describes sixty-four changes, or oracles, that are represented by hexagrams and deal with understanding every permutation of how to live an exemplary life in a practical spiritual sense. The last two hexagrams, "Before Completion" and "After Completion," are reversed chronologically so the book ends on a hopeful note. Before Completion becomes the last hexagram, illustrating how all life is cyclical, which is to say there is no beginning and no end. Remaining fluid, accepting change as the only absolute, is a key to becoming an exemplary being.

A fluid state of mind is the only remedy for the hose dilemma. No matter how careful I am to roll it up neatly or unroll it slowly, the hose puts up a fight. When I yank and get angry, it gets worse. The hose scrunches in a place I can't see or wraps itself around an obstacle, stopping its flow. The harder I pull, the tighter the constriction becomes. Is this beginning to sound like a metaphor?

Some people say the only answer is a drip system. This eliminates having to deal with the hose and is a more efficient way to water, both in terms of delivery and water supply. However that may be, I am an old-fashioned girl. I think watering is the most satisfying ritual of gardening. I don't want a drip system. I anticipate watering at the end of a planting as I would a special dessert at the end of a meal. A drip system would rob me of the tranquility I receive when I am experiencing the pleasure of quenching my garden's thirst.

I imagine the hose to be my umbilical cord to the earth. It is through the hose I feel something coming back to me from the plants. I am receiving nourishment, too. It is another one of those times in my garden that I disappear. My gray matter relaxes, watching the leaves brighten in the same way I do after a nice hot

shower, after having removed the residue of the day before. I breathe in the woodsy smell as the water soaks
deep into the soil. Watering refreshes like a walk in the
woods or a swim in a mountain lake. I recommend watering to anyone with a sensitive nervous system, and
these days I'm sure that includes a good number of us.

Modern life is jarring, to say the least. We all need an
outlet, a way to relax, recharge, and restore our equilibrium. The *New York Times* ran an article recently about a
nationwide architectural association that advocates
building hospitals with attached gardens so that patients
have a green landscape to look out on instead of an urban canyon. Studies have shown that Alzheimer's patients who are placed in a garden all day are no longer
violent. This statement is remarkable in its simplicity and
power. In the not too distant past, the healing power of
gardens was a matter of course. European sanitoriums incorporated time in their gardens as an essential part of
the cure. It is only with modern medicine's dependence
on taking a pill that we have lost the belief in healing
through osmosis by basking in the presence of nature.

I use watering as an excuse to meditate. Instead of
viewing watering as a time-consuming hassle that I
must rush through, I consider it to be the indulgence of
a sensual pleasure. I visualize the water as it percolates
downward below the surface. I sense a sigh of relief
from the plants and the dry earth as the water perme-
ates every corner and crevice, indiscriminately flowing
wherever it is accepted.

All this focusing contributes spirit to the garden. Before
the onslaught of modern civilization, people didn't have to
do meditations to bring them close to the earth and the

cosmic rhythms. Some Native Americans, for example, made love in the cornfields to generate fertility, both for the corn and for themselves. The umbilical cord to Mother Nature had not yet been severed. Oneness with the earth constituted a rich part of everyone's life and was associated with food, sex, love, ritual, religion, soul, and health.

Today we need to rehabilitate ourselves to see the earth not as an abstract concept, but as an intrinsic part of our own selves. The most magical aspect of having this awareness is that it can be nurtured in the privacy of your own home and by merely caring for houseplants. One does not need to have an outdoor garden to develop a feeling of oneness with the earth. Caring for a plant and watching it grow contains within it all the intricate possibilities and paradoxes of the entire universe.

When I water my garden, I water myself. It is a nurturing, cleansing, relaxing experience. The plants come clean, build moisture around themselves, and absorb a part of me. I learn to respect the lubricative quality of water and work on cultivating a fluid mind. As the opening passage from the *Tao-te Ching* states, water is flexible and has no resistance. It flows everywhere. Not a bad example to follow as we make our way in the world.

Lao-Tzu, accredited by most to be the author of the *Tao-te Ching*, taught extremely ancient principles in this book of wisdom that was written circa 550 B.C. The *Tao-te Ching* offers a way to clarify who we are and how to deal with life.

> If you want to shrink something, you must first allow it to
>   expand.
> If you want to get rid of something, you must first allow it
>   to flourish.

If you want to take something, you must first allow it to be
given.
This is called the subtle perception of the way things are.

The soft overcomes the hard.
The slow overcomes the fast.
Let your working remain a mystery.
Just show people the results.

Allowing yourself to be yourself, the natural you
without pretense and "shoulds," is the freedom that the
garden bestows. Empathy for the plants develops naturally. Empathy is the vessel through which I water my
garden. I know whether a plant needs water without
even touching the soil. From across a crowded room, I
am drawn automatically to a plant that is thirsty. The
leaves don't even have to be drooping. My body gets a
sense of the plant's dryness and demands that I give water to the thirsty plant. I feel the pull and follow it.

Just as you learn to read a dog's message that he or
she is thirsty, you can do the same with plants. After
you spend some time observing and being with your
plants in a focused way, you will gradually anticipate
their needs. Connecting to your plants, even one
plant in a pot, is a refinement of feeling your connection to "the earth." Plants in containers are not separate from the earth. They are a microcosm of the
larger entity of the planet. It is all connected.

EIGHT

A Tree Story in
Three-Part Harmony

*I like trees because they seem more resigned to the way they have to
live than other things do.*

—Willa Cather

Plants teach us about the human condition, what it means
to be fully human. Pets do the same thing. When you grow
to love another being, you open yourself to loss. Until
plants became important in my life, my emotional bonds
had been limited to people and pets. Now I was learning I
could include plants, too.

It is easy to become oblivious to the interconnectedness
of all life, even if you don't want to. I didn't know I was
well on my way until I saw my first tree die next door to an
apartment house I stayed in when I first left New York and
moved to Santa Monica, California.

The tree was a very old, thickly trunked date palm, a
Phoenix canariensis, that rose sixty feet into the air, with

about a fifty-foot spread. Even though it wasn't on my property, it shaded me. The light dappled through its enormous fronds recalling Matisse in Nice and luncheon on the grass in Monet's garden.

One day, I heard workmen planning to demolish the other house. A new apartment building was going up in its place. Too bad, I thought. The neighborhood will surely change. It never occurred to me what that might entail and how soon it would happen.

A week later, I came home to find the date palm cut to the ground, lying on its side like a dead elephant, a sleeping Buddha in the Sri Lankan forest. Slowly dying, severed from its core, it sprawled on the sidewalk outside my house, just one block from the busy traffic on Santa Monica Boulevard.

I stood frozen, watching the tree. I swear I saw it heave and heard it sigh. The dismaying sight of the date palm lying in state on its urban deathbed triggered feelings of sadness and powerlessness so disturbing, I instinctively buried them immediately.

Ten years later, in Bishop, California, while living in the house with the garden that produced the late-blooming cosmos, I got to know another tree. A one-hundred-year-old cottonwood tree played palace guard outside my bedroom window.

From my bed, I could contemplate the cottonwood tree. Life was quiet enough to hear the wind's peculiar rustle as it blew through the cottonwood's heart-shaped leaves. Soon, I noticed the sound came up at the same time every day, and I waited for it as I would the noon whistle. At night, peeking through the tree's silhouette, I saw my first meteor showers. While I paid bills at my desk or carried out business over the telephone, it refreshed me to glance up at the tree and allow its peaceful, reassuring presence to wash my brain so I could continue to concentrate.

The cottonwood provided a soothing reference point from everywhere on the property. As soon as I drove in, I felt welcomed. When I left, I knew it would be there when I returned. It towered over the neighborhood like a living green Sphinx and seemed to impart a peaceful feeling to everyone who came under its influence.

One night, it appeared in my dreams. I was standing underneath it examining its impenetrable form when two very sad brown eyes appeared in its trunk and stared back at me. I reached out to touch its face and the eyes disappeared. When I awoke the next morning, I felt as if something monumental had happened. I had been given a glimpse of the mythical nature of the tree.

I began to look differently at everything around me: the smattering of white phlox over by the side door, the hint of French lilac off in a corner, and the creamy Chinese snowballs gracing the north wall. Because of the dream, I took less for granted. I became more grateful.

The one eyesore, from my point of view, was the landlords' motor home parked on the concrete slab next to the entrance to the vegetable garden. I pretended, as best I could, that it wasn't there. The rest of the view was so pas-

toral. The motor home was my one reminder that the end
of the twentieth century was near and I was only one step
ahead of it, in my eternal search for a preindustrial landscape in which I could rest, be quiet, and think.

One day, the landlady nonchalantly mentioned she
wanted to cut down the cottonwood tree. She was convinced the tree was rotten at its core and needed to be elim-
inated from the yard so it wouldn't fall onto their motor
home or into my bedroom window. I thought she was jok-
ing. I even laughed, assuming the very thought of cutting it
down was as absurd to anyone else as it was to me. It was
inconceivable that she actually believed it was dangerous.

She had just bought the house two years before, having moved out of Los Angeles to avoid the traffic and
noise. Others who had lived in the neighborhood a long
time said the most reputable tree trimmers in the valley
had pruned the tree a year or two before she moved in.
They had declared it in excellent condition. All it needed
now, the neighbors said, was a good trim so its branches
wouldn't fall in undesirable places.

The landlady told me one more time she was contacting
tree trimmers for estimates on the removal of the cottonwood tree. Whoever agreed with her contention that the
tree was rotten inside won the deal. The company that
wanted the task obtained a lucrative job but took on a formidable mission. The roots were so old they spread high
above the ground throughout the yard, and so thick they
looked like electric train tracks traversing the far reaches of
the lawn. There was no doubt in anyone's mind they ran
underneath the foundation of the house, as well.

The stupid part of me kept denying the reality of what the landlady said she was going to do. There was no doubt in my mind she would come to her senses and opt for the luxurious green canopy that lowered the temperature in our little pocket ten degrees in the summer.

A month or two passed and I drove to Palm Springs for Easter week to see my mother who was visiting from New York. It was a tiring seven-hour ride home, and I was looking forward to sitting under the breezy green fortress of the cottonwood and sipping a cool drink.

As I drove in, I knew something was wrong. The first thing I saw were gargantuan rounds of tree trunks stacked haphazardly everywhere. There was no yard left. Every inch of it was filled with sections of the cottonwood tree. There was no way these rounds could be moved except by crane. They were perfectly formed with no trace of rot. All that was left of the tree was a giant stump.

There were men everywhere lifting wood and cutting with chain saws, cursing that poor tree with the foulest language for being such a bitch to cut down. One guy told me the tree had put up a hell of a fight. The tree cutters were exhausted and angry.

I stumbled around the rubble in shock as if Hiroshima had just happened in the backyard. I wanted to grab everyone and scream at them to wake up to the senselessness of what they had done. I finally realized there was nothing to do or say. I walked into my house and shut the door, closing all the blinds, and didn't come out for three days.

I bargained for a resurrection. I imagined the magnificent cottonwood tree miraculously pulling itself back together again, as things did in animated cartoons, and standing whole and vital once more. For a few moments, I actually believed this supernatural event might occur.

Two days later, more men arrived to load the rounds on a mammoth truck bed and haul them away from the scene of the crime. I peeked outside through a slit in the blinds. The landlady wanted them to scoop out the stump with a special power tool so she could use it for a flower bed. She had hoped the men would be able to remove the stump, but they couldn't. It was too huge and the roots too pervasive. Instead, the vestige remained, a sore reminder of its refusal to leave.

I experienced all the stages of grief during those first few days. In the beginning, denial and bargaining were the only way I could cope. Anger and resentment consumed me. Finally, I accepted that the nurturing two-year alliance with the cottonwood was over. I opened the blinds and looked out at the garden.

Breathing in deeply, summoning my courage to deal with the freshly cut stump, I walked outside. After sweeping my hands across the raw wood, I lay down on the stump's massive circumference and mourned for the tree's life, for the messed-up state of the world, and for my loss.

In a few days, friends and neighbors stopped by, proclaiming there was no rot in the wood; the tree had died in vain. I felt worse hearing such pronouncements. People inspected the stump and went away shaking their heads. The cottonwood had shaded such a large area, in its absence the yard now looked like an abandoned lot even though the rest of the garden was still intact.

At the time, I kept thinking, there must be something here I'm supposed to learn, trying to absorb the shock of another big tree felled right outside my house. Although I didn't know what it meant, at least this time I didn't bury it. I felt the blow. Four years later, in Laguna Beach, California, another tree would break through.

Laguna is a place where lush vegetation graces winding, tucked-away streets; homes are perched à la the French Riviera on hillsides; and the rocky coastline teems with hardy native shrubbery. Once the mecca for early California painters during the first few decades of the twentieth century, this beach community has a natural, picturesque quality, strewn as it is with stands of giant eucalyptus and smatterings of old California palms.

As it happened, while I was writing this book I needed to move in a hurry, actually in a matter of days. I didn't have time to look for a place. My friends Joan and Larry offered me their mobile home in Laguna to rent. At first I was snobbish about living in a trailer, but this old one was special. It looked like a boat inside.

Joan and Larry had gutted the interior to make one large studio space, salvaging the old wood paneling and white-washed indoor porch. A brand new kitchen served as the center around which the entire house revolved. Sliding glass doors and big picture windows opened out to a spacious deck and a one-hundred-and-eighty-degree view of the Pacific Ocean. From there I had full visibility of the curvature of the earth. Wherever I looked, there was the horizon, that hazy line between the conscious and the unconscious.

The deck became my garden. A fifty-foot California fan palm (*Washingtonia robusta*) stood directly in front of it. Immediately upon awakening in the morning, I'd go out and make my rounds to check on all the plants, and then sit in a chair and be with the tree.

Several different levels within its giant crown seemed to serve as a bird apartment house. I had a great view of the birds flying back and forth, singing and shrieking, playing tag, and generally having a ball. Watching the interrelationship of earth and sky and birds and sea made me feel like I had roots.

Two months after I moved in, my mother, Nina, came to visit. It was the first time she had ever stayed with me in my own home. We had a difficult history, a stalemated love-hate relationship involving a rift that must have occurred at birth. At that time, I was taken away from her and placed in an incubator for nine weeks, not to be removed for holding or touching. Instead, the medical staff poked, prodded, needled, and cut me trying to save my life. Being a mere two-and-a-half pounds with two external malignant tumors on my head, they attached me to a special tube for air and food; the box became my nurturer.

Naturally, none of this was my mother's fault. It kept me alive, but it must have been the early isolation and sensory deprivation that created a hunger which could never be satisfied. A chronic sense of neediness affected all aspects of my life: my work, my relationships, my health, and the most far-reaching, my self-respect. I grew up thinking life was pain and pain was life.

My mother seemed perpetually angry, and from my point of view it seemed I was the reason for her unhappiness. We played out a psychic dynamic in which I felt unloved and then, in my hurt and rage, gave her every reason to reinforce that feeling. After working on our ambivalent relationship for many years, we had finally begun to make progress. Even though we were still guarded, at least we were both facing in the same direction.

A few weeks earlier, I had visited my mother in Palm Springs. She traveled out to California each year from New York to vacation in the wintertime. While my stepfather was alive, the desert air helped his emphysema. After he died, my mother kept coming to escape the New York City winters and to see me. Even though we talked regularly on the telephone, a full year had passed since we had seen each other last. We got along so well, I decided to invite her to visit me a few weeks later, for her seventy-seventh birthday.

Five years before, while my stepfather was dying, my mother developed Parkinson's disease. With medication, she had been maintaining pretty well and was still able to take care of herself and get around. But after she arrived in California this year, she started to have a great deal more difficulty with her motor abilities. She lost her balance often, having trouble doing anything with her hands, getting up from a chair, or propelling herself out of bed.

It was painful to watch her being consumed by a rigidifying and progressively degenerating illness. My mother, who had always been strong and capable, who had never been sick, now could barely perform such simple tasks as putting on her shoes and socks, rifling through her purse for a credit card, or signing her name. Sometimes she would get this blank look on her face—the Parkinson's mask, or flat affect—and suddenly she wasn't there anymore. Her eyes went dead and she just stared vacantly, looking at once belligerent and afraid.

But even though my mother's body was hardening, her manner had softened considerably. She seemed sweeter to me since the onset of her illness. It made me wish the block between us would disappear

The morning after her arrival, we ate breakfast on the deck and began to hear the sound of a very loud and persistent chain saw, the kind tree trimmers use. I scanned the oceanfront and saw a man high up in a palm tree, way off in the distance, trimming the fronds. "It's spring," I thought. "It's nesting time. He's disturbing all the birds." Later, I would learn that this was precisely the idea.

After I washed the dishes, I looked out and saw men cordoning off the street. I called out to my mother, "Mom, it's going to be really loud in here in a minute." I started to get an uncomfortable feeling. There was bird panic around the palm tree. They were evacuating.

I didn't approve of this random destruction of their home, even though severe pruning of these gorgeous palms is a common practice in California. I recoiled from the deafening sound of the chain saw, retreating to my room to make the bed. I assumed the men would be trimming the fronds. Suddenly I heard my mother yelling over the din, "Look, look at what they're doing."

I hurried outside to the deck and looked up. The tree trimmer was only halfway up the palm. He wasn't cutting the fronds at all. He was cutting deep notches into the trunk to fell the tree. At first, it didn't compute. I looked at the notches and saw that it was too late to stop it. They were already cut too deep. The tree was about to fall any second.

Almost involuntarily, I started calling out, "Stop, stop! What are you doing? You can't do that. There's nothing wrong with that tree. Why are you doing this?"

The man just laughed at me. He obviously thought I was some kind of kook. He said, "Look, lady, I'm just doing what I'm told." The scene became surreal. The next thing I knew, there was a huge cracking sound. The trunk split and fell in slow motion directly toward me. It acted like a laser beam moving through the air, an invisible ray piercing the central axis of my body.

I will never forget the image of that palm tree falling directly into me as if it were going to split me in two. The tree trimmer had calculated exactly how much space it needed to land safely and miss my deck. Just a few more feet and the tree would have felled me.

My chest felt as if the tree had just performed psychic surgery on it, cutting me wide open and exposing my insides to the elements. Symbolically, a colossal wrecking ball had just whacked me to smithereens, and all my parts piled up in a heap neatly at my feet. The tree had cracked my armor, and grief poured out of me like a rising tide of water that had been dammed up for years.

Searching for some sense of control, I remembered the

hamadryads of Greek myth. The Greeks believed that a wood nymph, a tree spirit, lives inside each tree and is bound up with the life of that tree. When the tree dies, the hamadryad's spirit is released. I liked to think it was happening now so I could explain the situation and feel better. In an odd sort of way, it brought some comfort.

The lower half of the tree still stood. The top half, with its bushy head, lay slain in the street. The tree trimmer cut down the rest of the tree, chunk by chunk. This was the part of the process I had missed with the cottonwood. The noise drove me nuts knowing what it was doing.

I called the park office. "Why are you cutting down this tree?" I questioned.

"What tree?" she said.

"What tree?" I gasped, flabbergasted. "The one outside my house." I tried to calm down and put myself in her position listening to some crazy woman overreacting about a tree. After all, she must be thinking, "It's only a tree."

"Oh, yeah," she said. "That one. It's a shame, isn't it?"

"A shame," I cried. "Why? Why did you do it?"

"Well, we were getting so many complaints about other palms in the park. In the spring during nesting season, people complain bitterly about the bird droppings. Sometimes it gets so bad, the ground underneath becomes totally white."

"You mean you cut down the tree to prevent bird droppings?" I said incredulously. "I would have hosed down the street if you had told me." I hung up the phone in a daze.

It was then I noticed something changing in my body. It was an actual physical sensation. My chest tingled as if a numbness was wearing off. I had the odd feeling that something had been released.

My mother and I left the house and went to the beach to escape the noise. It was hard watching her get in and out of the car in slow motion. Her muscles wouldn't do the job anymore. I had to pull her up to give her some leverage so she could propel herself out of the seat. When she did it, I'd cheer for her and we'd laugh.

She shuffled slowly to the water's edge, her feet swollen and twisted from the Parkinson's. I laid her down on the blanket and she tried to make herself as comfortable as possible. We relaxed for a while, enjoying the waves breaking on the beach and the late afternoon sun warming us. "It's time to take a pill," she announced, as she often did every three hours or so.

Her life now consisted of taking five different kinds of medication and, in spite of great effort, she lost track of what she took when. Everything she did took triple the amount of time it normally might. I noticed I was becoming irritated by her slowness and inability to manage. It was almost easier to feel anger than to allow myself to feel the pain of how sad her decline was becoming for both of us.

She could still tell great stories but she forgot words and phrases. She'd stutter on words and fail to remember what she wanted to say. While we sat on the sand, my mother confided, in a shy sort of way, that the large dosage of medication she was taking caused hallucinations, yet she needed the higher dosage to keep her functioning. She mentioned nonchalantly that there was a very sweet doggie on the edge of the blanket and two large pussycats under the umbrella. When I asked if they scared her, she said, "No, they're company for me."

I had the sense that day, for the first time, that my mother was going to die. Maybe not in the next year or two, but we didn't have all that much time left. My mother had always been an essential part of my life. We may have fought a great deal but at least we talked, we were honest. Our relationship was alive. We even had our moments. Until now, though, I don't think I ever really entertained the idea of her being gone.

Watching her become like a little child, a sweet little girl who needed me to cut the food on her plate, made me see that my mother was shrinking away, both literally and figuratively. Still, a hard wall of stiffness, almost like a tree's trunk, blocked her expression of herself. We both were like tree trunks, she and I. We each had our own hard crust.

When my mother became too uncomfortable at the beach, I lifted her up and held her hand, and we walked slowly back to the car to go home. We ate Chinese takeout by the window in front of the absentee palm and hardly talked.

The next day was Sunday. My mother was scheduled to leave. When I awoke at 6:00 A.M., I felt a pressing desire to be physically close to her. She was already awake, so I walked over and sat on the edge of her bed, not knowing exactly what it was that I wanted to do.

I gave into my urge. I leaned over, pressed my heart against her heart, and started to cry. I asked her to forgive me for being so mean to her all my life and apologized for tormenting her with my rage.

After spending so many years blaming her for being such a lousy mother, I saw that she had given me everything she had to give. I had been condemning her for having a cold heart, for not loving me, for being critical and harsh, and now I was finally able to admit the part *I* played in that perception. I had been at least as cold, critical, and harsh as I ever accused her of being.

The spell had been broken. Our lifelong feud was over. We had arrived at the confluence of so many factors that catalyzed our healing: the shock of the tree's death, my mother's advancing illness, the efforts she had made to make our relationship work, the steps I had taken to reach the point of receptivity. We both were ready.

As we packed her bag together, making sure she knew where everything was, I helped her put on her underpants and snap her bra. I realized her helplessness didn't irritate me anymore. As I knelt on the floor by the bed putting on her socks, she volunteered, "The tree gave us a gift, you know. It gave us a new life together." My mother was all forgiveness. She had no rancor and I know she had reason. Her face looked as it did when I was a little girl. She looked young.

Now that my defenses had been cracked and I dropped the baggage I had been lugging around for years, I could see and appreciate the best of my mother. I could give her the same benefit of the doubt that I would afford anyone else. I stopped being vengeful and felt compassion instead. The fan palm had opened my heart. It had completed the work the other two trees had begun.

Trees don't argue or move or fight back. They endure their lot. My mother was enduring hers. We said good-bye, and after the car pulled away, I walked out onto the deck to be with the tree, momentarily forgetting it wasn't there. So, I sat in my usual chair, staring at the water, until the sun went down and the sky turned red.

I remembered in the past I might have been doing something or saying something and suddenly I'd feel I *was* my mother. I'd observe myself with her grimace, look askance with her smile, and I'd be spooked. I didn't want to be my mother. I was too afraid to look at the parts of her that I hated and admit them in myself. Now I know I am my mother, all parts of her. At this point in my life, I don't know anyone I would rather be.

It wasn't until a few days later that I realized I no longer had physical pain. I couldn't remember a day in the past fifteen years when I wasn't battling major pain in my body. Lower back problems, slipped discs, and severe sciatic pain had kept me bedridden and incapacitated, on and off, for years. Now, imperceptibly, the pain had ebbed away. I had let it go.

About two weeks later, I went to a local discount home emporium for some bamboo reed fencing to shade the area around my deck so my plants wouldn't burn up from too much sun. Usually, I don't frequent this certain store because the plants they sell look sick. But I wasn't going for plants this time. At least that's what I thought.

As I walked around the store looking for the fencing, sitting out in the aisle like a lost puppy in the pound, far away from the other plants, I spied a three-foot fan palm similar to the one that had died. The jolt of recognition was palpable. Bam! It was as if the plant was calling out to me, loud and clear, "Here I am for you. Take me home. A replacement for the deceased one."

Leaping at the chance, I hurried down the aisle and scooped it up into my arms, placing it possessively into the cart. The price tag read $13.99. What a deal on top of everything else! At this point, I was so overjoyed to see it, I would have bought it for any price.

The woody roots bulged out of the holes at the bottom of the black plastic pot. There was no doubt it had to be repotted immediately. I picked out a simple Italian terra-cotta pot and grabbed a bag of potting soil. Then I found a small wooden platform on wheels with a sliding dish underneath it to catch the run-off water so the carpet wouldn't rot.

I dragged the palm with me all over the store, treating it like I would a young child, not wanting to leave it alone for a minute. I found the bamboo fencing and headed for the checkout line. Bragging to the cashier about the fan palm's fabulous price, I hurriedly left the store, fully expecting her to follow me to say there had been some mistake.

I fitted the palm into the front passenger seat of my car, grateful there was enough room for it to spread out. I talked to it, telling it how wonderful I thought it was that I had been given a fan palm substitute, a sister-brother-child-cousin to the one who died.

When I got home, I excitedly repotted the palm. Its unusually vibrant green fronds spread out like beautiful ladies' hands. You could see the webbing between its fingers. I went to bed happy and lighthearted for the first time since the demise of the tree.

The next day I awoke to the smell of fresh, clean air, sweetened after a night of rain. I walked into the living room to discover that the fan palm had literally doubled in size overnight. The love, the water, the fresh soil and a place of honor in a new home, all combined to increase the vitality and size of the plant. The palm had swelled to a new height and stretched its arms out languidly in every direction, hanging as gracefully as a Victorian parlor palm.

My identification with the fan palm became clear. I had been a pot-bound root ball, too, stuck in the same childhood pot my entire life. In my case, it took cracking the whole container to set me free. I had been tugging for years, but I couldn't come out until I was absolutely ready. Now I flourished just like the palm.

Here I was, forty-seven years old, and I had finally grown up. At last I felt like a mature woman, taking full responsibility for my life. Inner gardening had become as rewarding as outer gardening was pleasurable. Growing myself was the gift from my garden.

NINE

Applying Inner Gardening

Never go to a doctor whose office plants have died.

—Erma Bombeck

By applying an inner perspective to gardening, you can add a new dimension to seemingly mundane gardening tasks such as watering, pruning, transplanting, and feeding. Perceiving gardening chores from a more sensitive point of view may change how you perform them. One of the greatest virtues of gardening is that the gardener is always learning. Discussing failures is an acceptable parlance among gardeners. Failure is part of the game. Once you see that the fun of gardening is doing, and then watching what happens, the pressure of goal-oriented gardening disappears.

Gardening forces you to be in the moment, to deal with what is happening in the here and now. Plants can't fake it like human beings can. They don't tell you everything is fine if it isn't. That's why observation is the single most useful talent to cultivate. Plants can sit neglected for long periods of time and neither die nor grow, but rather stagnate, through a gardener's lack of observation. I see plants, for example, that are plunked down in someone's dark hallway to cheer it up but instead make you want to cry, they look so pathetic. Being sensitive and observant means really looking at your plants. How do they make you feel? If you feel good when you look at them, it is likely they are healthy. If you feel sorry, your heart sinks, or you are repulsed, it is a good indication the plant is not happy.

By observation, I mean *feeling* as well as seeing. With patience, you can begin to *feel* your plants. At first, this may sound foreign, but think about how you use this function with people. We often talk about first impressions, and how we *feel* about a man or a woman upon meeting them. We derive that feeling from something coming to us from them. When people are angry, you can feel it, even if they have a smile plastered on their face or they say there is nothing wrong. Apply this ability to *feel* beyond surface appearances when you relate to your plants.

The bottom line assumption here is that you *want* to take care of plants. Plants will not stay looking like the day you bought them by themselves. They must be cared for. They are living beings that need the same things we do: food, air, water, and love. They need grooming such as cleaning, cutting back, and the removal of dead leaves. Plants thrive on attention and nurturance, just as any adult, child, mammal, bird, fish, rodent, or reptile. Plants just happen to be the lowest on the food chain, and we are not used to treating them with the same respect we give other sentient beings. Changing the attitude is vital, but it is only half the story. If you want plants, *you have to take care of them*.

This care does not mean you have to become a slave to your plants unless, of course, you become a slave of love. Be advised, gardening can become addictive. After that first charge of watching your plants grow in direct response to your care, usually you will want to grow more. It is possible, though, to maintain an indoor or outdoor garden that gives you great pleasure and is manageable, too, in terms of time and labor.

Start small and expand slowly so you are not overwhelmed in the beginning and then give up out of frustration and failure. Before you load up on houseplants, or clear the way for a huge outdoor garden, see if you enjoy doing it first. Start playing with one or two plants. Be realistic about how much time and effort you want to devote to helping them grow. The more energy you give them, the more abundant the reward. This axiom is the secret to successful gardening.

The truth is, a little water and a lot of attention go a long way. You don't even have to know that much to enjoy a flourishing garden. A garden gives. That is its nature. Once you begin to garden, you will be pleasantly surprised to see the many ways in which this happens. Plants provide unconditional love. The enchantment of plants, in all their myriad forms, is the hook of gardening. Plants have dignity and presence. Every time I see a huge palm tree transported on a flatbed truck, I notice its dignity. It lies there, out of its element, bouncing up and down, yet it still emanates a distinct and intelligent existence.

People who are sensitive to the interconnectedness of all life are often driven to despair by the callous way plants are treated. I have seen bougainvilleas blooming magnificently on my morning walk, and the next day the owner will have clipped it to shreds with an electric trimmer, all in the name of pruning it. Part of this prune-happy problem is financial. When I talk to park managers and homeowners who hire gardening help, they say it's cheaper to pay for one drastic pruning than a few minor ones. But, a hack prune job lacks sensitivity and respect. Besides, it's ugly.

Plants have beauty in every stage of the life cycle. Try watching a plant unfold naturally throughout its entire cycle of growth. We are so used to expecting everything to look "good" all the time. Instead of pulling out plants as soon as they look a little bit past their peak, try to develop a new aesthetic. Let the lettuce go to seed and see its flowers bloom. The personality of the plant manifests itself differently in each of its forms: roots, leaves, buds, flowers, fruit, seeds, and all the gradations in between.

Recently, I planted a bundle of mixed sunflower seeds that my gardening friend Jennifer gave me. I planted them in a circle around my tiny garden plot in front and alongside the entrance to my house. About eighty sunflowers came up. Some of them grew to be more than seven feet high. Most had giant faces, some with dark flat centers, others with domed yellow centers, and many had auxiliary flowers that jutted out in different directions off the main stem.

Until I grew my own, I had no idea that a heavenly scent emitted from their core. The smell was so sweet I could imagine what it did for the bees that came and got drunk in their yellow pollen. Every morning, I couldn't wait to go out and inhale the fresh sugar from the sunflower faces and let them brush pollen all over my nose.

A cheerful sight, these bumper-to-bumper sunflowers attracted bravos from motorists, joggers, and walkers. They made everyone happy. People drove by smiling, waving, and honking, pointing at the sunflowers. The flowers peaked for about a month and then they hung their heads, huge yellow petals rippled like wavy hair, each flower displaying its own personality and attitude. The flowers projected the same dignity in their bearing as trees. They posed like beautiful women in various stages of maturity, with a different kind of beauty from the perfection of their peak, but a beauty nonetheless.

I read an article once that suggested in American culture, we have come to expect life to unfold as one peak experience after another, just as in commercials where people are ecstatic—laughing and thrilling to their cars, their love lives, and their breakfast cereals—all the time. On the whole, commercials depict only peak experiences. The younger generation has come to expect life to be this way. Young people compare their lives to commercials and, naturally, they fall short. They become depressed and frustrated by their "lack of success" and assume everyone else has a life of uninterrupted bliss except them.

The same expectation and attitude permeate our thinking about plants and gardens. I come across people all the time who think their garden should always be blooming perfectly, and if it's not there is something wrong. But there is satisfaction and comfort in watching a plant go full circle.

I recently collected seed from my sweet pea flowers. For almost four months, they straddled the side wall of my deck in a curly mass of color, from violet, magenta, and lavender to reds, pinks, whites, and fuchsia. Their abundance and distinctive haunting fragrance gave me so much pleasure, I decided to let the vines die off and go to seed, even though part of me wanted to cut down the finished flowers so I wouldn't have to look at a mess. I still had the voice that said I should keep everything looking perfect. It's better not to have any plant, than one that is not perfect. But I really wanted to collect the seeds so I could reproduce the same event next season, and give the seeds to friends so they could enjoy them, too. I spent at least a month watching the vines turn brown.

After a while, the brown vines and seed pods grew on me. I began to understand in my gut what is meant by the integrity of the plant. The wholeness of its agenda became apparent. When I opened my first pods, the peas shone like black sapphires, luminous, with such a profound concentration of life. In the simple act of saving seeds for the following year, I connected with the earth and completed one entire cycle with a plant I loved. I took part in an ancient spiritual ritual commemorating life/death/rebirth. While picking the pods, removing the seeds, and placing them in a jar for storage, I felt the sweet pea oil rub off on my fingertips. When I plant them next year and the flowers come up, we will be old friends. On the day I cut down the vines and shelled the last pod, I actually found myself saying to the sweet peas, "Now I know you. I really know you."

Once you begin to care for plants, magic happens on its own. If you extend yourself to the invisible world, it will give back to you tenfold. Every time you make something beautiful, you are being invisibly helped. Once you become interesting to the spiritual world, it will show you more and more of itself. Clarifying your intent to the plants is the most helpful way to make contact. Once you have acknowledged you want to have a relationship with them, they will respond and show you their gratitude. You will build cooperation and trust. It doesn't happen right away. It takes time, just as it does with people.

A friend rescued a Christmas poinsettia from the garbage at her work. Never having even considered taking care of plants before, this act was a big step for her, especially since the plant had been reduced to a brown, woody stem. But, she watered it and cared for it and let it know through her actions that she wanted it to live. Many new gardeners think the plant is dead when it looks like that, but actually there is tremendous dormant power lying in wait for the right touch. With just a tiny bit of care, a plant that looks terrible can end up flourishing. The plant grew bushy and green, much to my friend's surprise.

Inspired, she went on to plant a whole package of basil seed in a tiny pot. The entire time she kept thinking, these will never come up. She found herself excited when green sprouts emerged from the soil. The first time you see it happen, you experience the miracle that it really is. Now she wants to try something else. This woman didn't have any idea what she was doing, but she experimented to see what would happen and she was rewarded. Now she is ready for more. Which brings me to the best advice I can offer. Just do it. The learning is in the doing. A garden is a very loving and thorough teacher.

Water

Watering a garden is probably the best way to come down to earth. Plants need water. It is an inescapable fact. You cannot forget to water your plants and have them miraculously not droop. There is a point of no return beyond which they will not come back. I planted a mallow in a large terra-cotta pot on my deck. It liked frequent watering; otherwise it went limp. As the weather grew hotter, I didn't keep up with its needs. One day I came home to find it hunched over, hanging over the edge of the pot like a Raggedy Ann doll.

I talked to it, touching it gently, apologizing for my carelessness and lack of attention and asked it to please come back. I soaked the plant thoroughly and moved it into the shade. In a matter of minutes, the mallow began to raise itself to its full height again. I picked off the leaves that hadn't recouped, trimmed the tip growth that had turned brown, and the mallow looked healthy again.

Watering properly takes mindfulness. If you swing out of balance, you can be either a smothering parent or an irresponsible one. The smothering kind is worse. Overwatering is actually more of a problem than underwatering. When you overwater repeatedly, the roots will rot, destroying the foundation. Roots should be white. If you check the roots and they are orange or brown or soggy, they are not healthy. The plant takes in water and stores food through its roots. Once the roots decay, there is no chance of recovery. It is also true that if your roots are in good shape, but there is no sign of foliage, you can bring back the plant from nothing.

Keep in mind that you can never overwater by watering too much at one time. You can only overwater by watering too often. When you water plants that live in containers, make sure you do so until you see water coming out the bottom of the pot. Think you are putting water in a bank account which the plant can draw upon at its own pace. If you send water through a few times, it will insure a good soaking, and leave no dry pockets.

How much water a plant needs depends upon the amount of light it receives. If it gets a lot of sun, a plant needs a lot of water. If a plant sits in the shade, in a north window, or one with filtered light, it will not need as much water as the plant that sits in bright light. If the weather is very hot, the soil will dry out rapidly. Then, even though you think you've watered a plant, it will not receive all you gave it. Take these factors into consideration when you water.

Don't wait until the plant wilts before you water it. Wilting constitutes a trauma and exhausts the plant. You have fingers. They are your barometer. Touch the soil. Dig down a couple of inches to see if the plant is dry. If it is, soak it well and wait. Feel the soil in a few days and see if it's dry again. If it is, water. If not, wait. Be sure to stick your fingers down a few inches. The soil at the top can dry out, but if you go down a little farther, the soil can be wet.

Most plants prefer to dry out between waterings but ferns like to be kept moist all the time. It takes a while to get to know your plants. You will get a sense of their watering needs after caring for them for a few weeks. You can reach a point of intimacy with a plant when you won't even have to touch the soil to know if it needs water. You will feel it. You will sense it by its color and turgidity, or how robust or how drained it looks.

Do not allow your plants to sit in water. Their roots will rot. If there is still water in the dish when you have finished watering, spill it out. This can be tricky if you have a plant in a pot sitting within another pot, basket, or decorative container. Check these plants often to see their condition. I have seen many a plant become waterlogged because its feet are always wet.

One way to ameliorate the situation is to place pebbles or stones in the dish and rest the pot on top of them. You will still have to check to see that the water doesn't rise above the stones. The humidity that is created by the evaporation of the water in the rocks will lend moisture to the air around the plant. Particularly in centrally heated apartment houses or those heated by radiator, moisture is always welcome.

Leaves reveal how the plant is doing. If the leaves are crunchy, brittle, brown, or drop off, it is likely the plant is not getting enough water. But, these signs could also mean the plant is getting too much sun or is pot-bound. This is where touching the soil comes in. If the soil is still moist, then water is not your problem. If it's dry, when did you water last? Check to see how much sun the plant gets. Sometimes plants burn or bleach out in hot sun, especially those shoved up against windowpanes. You will have to weigh all the factors. Be a sleuth. Only you and the plant know what is really happening.

Ask for watering advice when you buy an indoor or outdoor plant. Always read the directions that are attached. Nurseries are in the business to help. Use them as a resource, especially if the plant comes without any instructions. Usually plants carry directions on light preference and water needs. Do not disregard these. They are an essential part of inner gardening. Plants cannot live on good vibes alone.

Since every garden is unique in its needs and situation, whatever you do, don't maintain a rigid watering schedule. There are too many variables to have rules such as water your plants three times a week, come what may. Relate to each plant as an integral part of your environment. This interaction is essential in getting to know your garden.

Use water that is a moderate temperature. Indoors, room temperature is best. Do not water with very cold water. It will shock the plants. Let water stand in a watering can or be sure it is tepid when taking it from the tap. Once, at the end of a party, I saw a woman pour a bucket of ice water into a potted palm. I suggested to her that chilling the plant like that might shock it. She disregarded the notion, saying the man at the nursery told her to put ice cubes on the soil when she went away for a few days. They would melt and provide water for the plants in her absence. Even though I am not crazy about this concept, there is a difference between a whole bucket of ice water and a few ice cubes. Use your discrimination. Ask yourself always, how would I feel if someone did this to me?

Although you may like hanging plants or those that cascade from high shelves, they can become the most difficult to keep alive. The air tends to be significantly hotter the higher up you go, especially in winter because of indoor heating and fires. When plants are hard to see and touch, checking them for dryness is difficult. A neglect syndrome develops when watering proves to be a messy business. Either you have to take down the plants every time you want to water them, or you must guess, and blindly water by hand. Often the water overflows onto the floor or carpet and you have to clean it up. This process becomes tedious very quickly, and you stop watering because it's just too much trouble. Then the plant suffers.

The plants that thrive are usually the ones that can be easily observed. Keep plants within your view and your touch. They need your attention, your glance, your rustle of their leaves, your feel of their soil. They love to be petted.

I recently moved a small rabbit's foot fern, just beginning to get on its paws again, into the house for rehabilitation. It was practically dead when I brought it home originally. I purchased it for fifty cents at the same fundraiser where I found the Medusa cactus. The fern loved the shade on my patio, but after I moved, the sun on my deck blasted it, draining its color and drying up its foliage. Finally, I decided to bring it indoors. I put the rabbit's foot on a bookshelf behind my maidenhair fern, thinking it would like the low light and a fellow fern. It just sat there doing nothing, looking stunted and graceless.

Theoretically, I put it in a good place, high atop the file cabinet in my office. Practically, I couldn't even touch the soil or see it up close without craning my neck and standing on my toes. At last it became apparent that I needed to place the fern in the plant clinic at the kitchen sink. There, the neediest plants receive my attention whenever I am in the kitchen, which is a lot.

I soaked the fern in the sink and primped its tiny fronds, silently welcoming it to the Baden-Baden of the plant set. By evening, the fern came alive again. I patted it whenever I passed by, and the rabbit's foot poufed accommodatingly in return. In one day, the entire demeanor of the fern changed. Such a noticeable response to a switch in care is always heartening. If something isn't working, try something else.

During the summer, plants dry out quickly, especially those in pots outside. And especially those in porous terracotta pots. When it is particularly hot, you may even have to water twice a day outdoors. After soaking the soil thoroughly, hose down the pot with water, as well as the area around the pot if it sits on anything other than earth or grass. Terraces, patios, and stairs, particularly those made of brick, concrete, or asphalt, can become like a hot skillet. This heat radiates to the plants unless you hose down the surfaces. You'll see when you do it, the water will sizzle and steam will rise.

In my opinion, drip systems do not adequately satiate

plants. They may conserve water and make it easier to care for your garden, but my experience with them has been unsatisfying. The feeling I get from most plants watered by the drip method is that they are deprived. They sort of maintain, but they don't thrive. If you do use a drip system, complete the watering process once in a while with thorough irrigation using automatically timed sprayers, or use your hands. You may have a positive experience with drip systems, but consider this. Hand watering is a tangible way to connect with your plants.

I understand many people think they don't have the time. I am suggesting that perhaps, if you are not watering by hand, there is a missing element to your gardening. Growers, producing on a mass scale, use automatic watering systems. But, if you have a small area, you might consider watering by hand as a sure way of bonding with your garden.

Light

Be aware of how you place your plants. They love to be together. The closeness of their foliage creates more humidity in the air around them. Plants seem to thrive when they are arranged in groups. If you watch them closely, you will see that they grow into one another, intertwining and closing ranks, so they can touch. After plants have been together for a while, they unite into a coherent whole, merging their individuality into the overall effect of the group. In your arrangement of plants, make sure each one is receiving the appropriate light.

Light is one of the most limiting factors in growing

plants. Often, you can fudge the requirements a little and grow full-sun plants in dappled light. But flowering plants usually need a few hours of sun a day or else they won't bloom. Without sun, sun-loving plants become weak and scraggly. Leaf loss and stagnation will follow. Remember what happened to the ficus?

Conversely, it is just as callous to place shade-loving plants in direct sun. When a plant overdoses from too much sun, it turns gray and limp or its leaves burn. Providing you haven't subjected it to such an assault for long, a plant's rich healthy color will return by moving it back into the shade. This may take a little time, but it will happen.

Gauge your light situation by identifying your exposure. Southern exposure means sun all day unless you have an obstruction like a tree or a building. Western exposure means afternoon sun. Afternoon sun is hotter than morning sun, the kind you receive from an eastern exposure. Plants that can't take too much sun will often wilt in afternoon sun but be very content in morning sun.

Northern exposure, the kind artists love for painting, gives bright light that casts no shadow. Most plants, except some flowering plants, will do very well in this light. Even cactus and succulents, which we think of as desert plants that adore sun, can be overwhelmed by too much. Their serene blue and lavender colors fade or turn yellow, or their fleshy leaves redden like a sunburn. If you don't have direct sun but do have bright light, you are actually in good shape. Except for vegetables and many herbs and flowers, which need direct sun, you can grow almost anything else with success in north light.

Air

Plants and trees purify our air as they produce their own food. They take in the carbon dioxide we exhale and give off oxygen. Through the green in their leaves, plants utilize the light energy from the sun and transform it into sugars, which are sent to the roots and to the tips of stems. This process is called photosynthesis. It is how plants make their own food since they can't go out and get it themselves. They manage this miraculous feat with a little help from their friends, the soil, the water, and the air.

A woman in one of my workshops had a plant that was dying in her living room. After we went through all the possibilities, I asked her where it sat. She said it lived in a basket in front of the fireplace. It turned out to be a gas fireplace, and even though a small amount of gas escaped from the pilot, it was enough to cause harm to the plant.

The same sort of thing happens with air conditioners. Plants do not like to sit in drafts. How do you feel after being in a cold draft? Your shoulder freezes up or your neck tightens and becomes stiff. Plants can get chilled, too. Touch their leaves. If they are cold, the plant is cold.

Most indoor plants are happiest at fifty-five degrees. Anything below this temperature becomes difficult for them. Keep this in mind during cold winter nights or if a plant sits touching a windowpane. Conversely, when the temperature rises and gets really hot, plants wilt. Then air-conditioning helps, as long as it isn't blowing on the plant.

Plants like air. Open your windows. They like the wind. It's natural for them. Plants enjoy swaying in the breeze and rustling in the wind. Air circulation is beneficial. Put your houseplants outside, once in a while, if you have a windowsill, stairway, fire escape, patio, terrace, or back-yard. Plants will especially appreciate sitting out in the rain. Warm or cool rain is best. Hail and snow will shock your hothouse buddies.

In 1989, NASA issued a final report on a study conducted at the John Stennis Space Center in Mississippi. In their report—"Interior Landscape Plants for Indoor Air Pollution Abatement"—they found that one potted plant per hundred square feet of floor space can help clean the air in the average home or office. (This gives you some idea of how important trees and plants are in our environment.) According to NASA, almost every tropical indoor plant, and many flowering plants, actually remove harmful indoor air pollutants found in a variety of household products, as well as in clothes and furniture.

The following list, published by the *Foliage for Clean Air Council* in Falls Church, Virginia, may encourage you to use indoor plants as air purifiers.

Pollutant	Source	Solutions
Formaldehyde	foam insulation	philodendron
	plywood	spider plant
	clothes	golden pothos
	carpeting	bamboo palm
	furniture	corn plant
	paper goods	chrysanthemum
	household cleaners	mother-in-law's tongue

Benzene	tobacco smoke	English ivy
	gasoline	marginata
	synthetic fibers	Janet Craig
	plastics	chrysanthemum
	inks	gerbera daisy
	oils	warneckei
	detergents	peace lily
Trichloro-ethylene	dry cleaning	gerbera daisy
	inks	chrysanthemum
	paints	peace lily
	varnishes	warneckei
	lacquers	marginata

The critics of this study question whether the airtight chambers of NASA's experiments translate to the home or office environment. They emphasize there is no research yet proving plants can do the same thing there. I say, you can't go wrong with plants in the house. The more, the better, as long as they are happily cared for and healthy. They clean the air, add moisture, provide natural beauty, and offer a connection to the Earth.

Cleaning, Grooming, Cutting Back, Pinching

Just as we take showers and cut our hair, plants need grooming, too. One can take a neglected patio, terrace, or backyard and turn it into a showplace in a few hours by grooming the plants. Indoors, grooming is especially important, since plants can get pretty depressing-looking if left to their own devices.

Many new gardeners think a few brown leaves mean the plant is dead. Unless the whole plant is brown, death is an unlikely diagnosis. More likely, it just needs grooming. Pick off the yellow, brown, or shriveled leaves; cut back unhealthy parts of the plant; and trim tips that have turned brown or yellow. Hose down or spray the leaves with plain water. It is surprising how good plants can look with just a little work. We are not talking about anything difficult, fancy, or costly.

In the natural growth process, leaves decay. If a plant has green healthy-looking new growth, you usually have no worries. But, discolored leaf tips can be a signal that the plant needs repotting. If there are roots coming out the bottom of the pot or the soil has turned into a solid root ball, this certainly means that repotting is your next step. (See the section on repotting for more direction.) If repotting doesn't seem to be in order, use scissors and trim the leaves, following their natural shape and fluid lines. Be artistic. A blunt cut can make a plant look clumsy.

Cleaning plants with a diluted solution of a nondetergent soap and water will help perk up a plant. Almost everywhere you go these days, the air is dirty. Soot and dust settle on the leaves of plants and the grime inhibits their intake of light, as well as their respiration and transpiration (giving off moisture through the pores in their leaves).

Spraying them with a solution of a drop or two of mild liquid soap in a quart of water breaks up the grime. Plants that are feathery or have tiny leaves will be happy with a good spray. Plants with broad leaves are easy to clean by wiping them with a sponge. You cannot do this too often. Only plants with furry or hairy leaves such as begonias, violets, and geraniums dislike water on their foliage.

Watch out for indoor plants sold at discount centers that sell things other than plants. My theory on these plants is that they have lost their soul. They are almost like plastic plants. They have been overbred in greenhouses and pumped up with growth hormones that make them look great when you buy them but don't last. After they are at your house for a while, they start to look sickly. It's not your fault. They have been treated artificially to grow.

To someone who is sensitive to plants, walking by these departments in discount stores is very sad. The plants feel as if they are from *The Invasion of the Body Snatchers*. Compare them to plants at a good nursery. The discount ones are clones. This is not to say you shouldn't buy these plants, but if you do, you will have to transmute the effects. They almost always need repotting. Use your fingers to loosen the soil from the root ball, a term I use loosely in this situation. Often, the roots will be either immature or pot-bound. Sometimes they will be potted in a growing medium such as perlite and vermiculite or just plain peat moss, with no soil at all. Shake this off and surround the roots with fresh soil.

If the leaves are excessively shiny and waxy, this means they have been treated with a plant polish to make them look healthy. In fact, this substance clogs their pores, inhibiting respiration and transpiration. A healthy plant will shine on its own. It does not have to be cosmetically enhanced to look beautiful. It's the old story, if you feel good, you look good. Remove the waxy buildup with a diluted solution of water and nondetergent soap. Use a sponge on the broad-leaved plants. Don't be afraid to rub.

Cutting back is a good practice when you notice a plant has become straggly or leggy. You know how good you feel when you get a haircut. It seems to revitalize your scalp and promote blood circulation in your head. The same thing happens with a plant. It sends the energy back down to the center of the plant and dormant buds become activated. Cutting back forces new growth all over and promotes bushiness.

At first it is hard to rationalize cutting back, particularly if there is new growth or flowers at the tips. But, a spindly plant will be grateful for a redirection of its energies. Be sure you give notice and discuss your intent.

When you cut back, always do so right above a node. Nodes are the bumps on the stems where the new growth forms. If you cut in between the nodes, naked stems will jut out and look unsightly. People often cut roses incorrectly. They don't cut back to a node and the naked stem turns brown above it and ruins the overall look of the plant. When you cut flowers, it is important to cut back just above a node. The same goes for all plants that branch.

Keep in mind that wherever you cut, the new growth will protrude from that point. Scan your plant carefully before you cut. Determine the shape you want your plant to have. Cutting back can give a whole new life to a sluggish plant.

Pinching is another way to redirect the growth of a plant. It does not work on plants that grow from a central core such as palms, dracaenas, and spiders. It does work wonders on vinelike plants and upright plants that have tip growth. The idea is to scoop out the newest growth at the tips, forcing the energy downward, to the parts of the plant closer to the soil. Pinching will create branching and new growth all over. You will get four new leaves for every two you pinch.

Use your thumb and forefinger to pinch out the tip growth. Do it before the new bud splits and becomes two, while the bud still appears to be one point. Sometimes if you pinch too late, the next generation of leaves will be slightly deformed. One may have a hole at the top or look as if something took a bite out of it. Don't think that you have ruined the plant. It will right itself in the next generation.

Pots, Potting, Repotting

If you are not planting in the ground, you need to use containers. Pots are the easiest containers to keep indoors. Outdoors you can use almost anything that will hold soil, such as wooden barrels, flower boxes, crates, metal artifacts, or decorative containers. Unless you are a seasoned gardener, it is best to use containers that have a hole at the bottom for proper drainage. Otherwise, you might have a hard time judging how much to water and end up with soggy soil and rotted roots. You can drill a hole if you are attached to a pot that lacks one. Or, you can use it as a decorative pot, placing a potted plant inside.

I have a spider plant that has been living for six years in a pot without a drainage hole and it flourishes. I really can't say how. As far as I am concerned, it's living on borrowed time. But I have grown accustomed to its habits, and a long time ago I asked it to adjust to its pot if it didn't want to come out. It wouldn't budge, but every time I share my concern about its health, it accelerates its growth.

The hole in the bottom of a pot needs to be covered with something, a piece of broken pot, or a stone or rock. This covering will prevent soil from running out the bottom when you water and regulate how fast the pot drains. If the pot has no drainage, build up a bottom layer with about an inch and a half of broken pot shards to create drainage space. The water that sits there will eventually evaporate. Include a few small pieces of charcoal. It will act as a filter or sterilizer so the stagnant water doesn't smell.

There are many pots to choose from, depending on your needs. My favorite are the porous terra-cotta pots that breathe, but many people prefer plastic ones. The soil in a clay pot will dry out faster, so watering more often is a must. But clay is made from the earth. It adds weightiness to container gardening. It's almost like putting a plant back into its own element. The Italian ones are more expensive and are of the highest quality. Some of the Mexican pots are sturdy and good looking, while other less expensive Mexican pots can disintegrate within a month. I've seen it happen. These pots can actually turn to dust before your very eyes. Even though they were cheap, I ended up spending more time and money replacing the pot and cleaning up the mess than I would have if I'd bought a more expensive one in the beginning.

There are different kinds of plastic pots. I have had difficulty growing anything in the ones made of a rubbery, softer plastic that are fashioned to resemble terra-cotta. Even though these pots have holes in the bottom, something is amiss with the material and its drainage. I have tried to plant in every size and shape pot, all with disastrous results. Everything from seeds to sets to shrubs slowly stagnated and died. I won't use these pots anymore. You may have a different experience.

The benefit of a high quality, hard plastic pot is that it will retain water longer than a clay pot. There is one drawback, however, that requires vigilance. Sometimes, the soil in plastic pots hardens and shrinks away from the edges of the pot. When you water, be careful that it doesn't fall into the crevices down the sides and run out the bottom of the pot. Water slowly, making sure it sinks into the soil each time you water.

Repotting needs to be done when there is no more room for the roots to spread. Usually you can tell this is happening when hardly any soil remains and the root ball has become one solid mass of white roots. It is always instructive to see how pot-bound a plant has become when you remove it from its old pot. The roots are so strong, you get a real sense of their power to lift sidewalks and break pipes

If you can see roots growing out the hole in the bottom of the pot, it usually means you need to repot. Use your fingers to loosen the soil at the top. If you feel a solid mass of roots, it's pot-bound. The sure way to tell is by tapping the root ball out of the pot so you can see the whole thing. Sometimes all that is left is a mass of roots in a tightly knit ball. Not a drop of soil falls from its grip.

Browning or yellowing around the edges of leaves can be a telltale sign of a pot-bound plant. Or, if you find you are having to water a plant much more often than usual, otherwise it goes limp, it could be pot-bound. It may also be that the foliage part of the plant has become top-heavy, meaning the plant looks out of proportion to the size of its pot. Sometimes plants become so top-heavy, they can't even stand up anymore. Then they keel over, pot and all. Obviously, you will be able to tell when this happens.

Before shifting to a larger pot, you may be able to buy time, perhaps even six months, by *shouldering* a plant, instead. This means you can "tickle" the root ball with your fingers and remove the soil, then trim the roots with a scissor, pruner, or sharp knife. This process is a reverse cutting back. Repot in the same container, adding fresh potting mix in the bottom and around the edges. Pack it down well and then water thoroughly.

Once you have decided to repot to a larger container, here are some basic guidelines. When you graduate to a new size pot, go up only one or two inches larger. If you repot a plant into too big a pot, the plant will spend all its energy filling up the soil with roots. You end up with a huge root ball and no top growth. Many plants like to be squeezed. That means if you contain their root ball in a smaller pot, the energy pushes upward, and the foliage fills out.

Measure the diameter across the top of the old pot before you buy a new one. If you have some extra pots lying around, experiment to see which one fits. Repotting is not difficult, although at first it may be scary trying to remove the pot-bound plant. Don't forget to give it notice and state your intent. Often, a plant is so ready, you can tug on it gently and it will lift right out of the pot. Other times, you may have to lay the pot on its side and tap around the sides to loosen the root ball. You can also use a knife to separate the root ball from the sides of the pot by sticking it down around the sides of the root ball as if you were cutting a circle into a cake. Whatever you have to do, be gentle and proceed slowly. Hold the plant with one hand so if it comes out of the pot suddenly, it won't fall on its foliage and break.

Prepare the new pot with soil *before* doing anything else. Have it ready. Use your eye to assess how high the plant needs to sit in the new pot. Fill the pot with soil less than halfway up. Tamp down the soil and let the plant rest on top. Judge how much higher or lower the plant needs to be. Center the plant in the pot so it sits comfortably and evenly. Fill in the leftover space with soil, holding on to the plant with one hand to keep it upright, if necessary.

The soil level will drop when you water. Be sure to tamp down the soil tightly in the pot. You may have to add soil after you water if the soil level drops too much. That's why tamping it down is important. Do not fill the pot all the way to the top. Leave a few inches so when you water there will be space, and the soil won't overflow.

Plants sometimes go into shock when their root ball has

been disturbed. You will know when your plant is in shock. It droops, goes limp, its color drains, and the leaves wilt. Giving notice will help prevent shock. Unless you have really butchered the root ball, most plants will come out of shock in a few hours or a few days, so don't throw it out! Bougainvilleas are notorious for being temperamental to repot or transplant. Their roots are extremely sensitive and the plant can die on the spot if the roots are disturbed. The best way to treat a plant in shock is to place it in the shade and water when it is dry. Don't demand anything of it. It needs time to gather its forces again. The same is true of any newly repotted plant. Keep it in the shade for about a week so it doesn't have to work so hard. Give it time to acclimate. Love and encourage it. Transitions are hard on everyone.

Support your plant. A problem can arise when a plant isn't doing well. You can grow to dislike it. Even hate it. Perturbed is the gardener who hates one of her plants. A scorned plant is a dead plant. The rare occasion does arise when benign neglect encourages a plant to thrive. But what I am describing is malignant neglect, disliking a plant to the point of mental cruelty. Then it is time for a divorce. Give away the plant to someone who wants it. Or change its appearance in some way so you can transcend your impasse with each other. Repot into a new container. Place it in another location that gives it a new look.

I did this with a large pot of nasturtiums on my deck. I love nasturtiums. That's why I planted them. But every time I looked at them, I got an ache in my chest. I didn't like the way they looked. Even though they overflowed the sides of the pot and cascaded wildly, which I liked, they grew in such profusion, brown and shriveled leaves multiplied amply each day. I picked off as many as I could, so the plant still looked reasonably healthy, but something was wrong and I couldn't figure out what. It certainly wasn't time to take them out. Maybe it was their color. They didn't fit in.

Finally, I decided to move the nasturtiums off by themselves against a white wall. Immediately, these orange nasturtiums assumed a whole new look. Juxtaposed to the white wall in the late afternoon sun, they could have been growing on the side of a barn in the country. After showing them off to a better advantage, I liked them again. A change of scene is even good for plants.

Feeding

Fertilizing is a touchy subject. There is a wide variety of opinion on the merits of feeding, as well as on the kind of food to give. As with everything else in gardening, if you read five books on the subject, you will have five schools of thought. Eventually you have to make all the advice your own and decide what works best for you.

Some people feed often and others almost never. The people who feed a lot say you need a regular and consistent feeding schedule to add nutrients to the soil. As long as you are moderate and regular in your feeding, it works. Unfortunately, many people have a "give me a pill" mentality when it comes to plant care. They assume there is a magic potion they can feed their plants and miraculously everything will be beautiful. Needless to say, this is fantasy. Plants need consistent watering, grooming, and feeding. If you do these three things, your garden will be beautiful.

I view chemical fertilizers as something akin to steroids. They pump up the plants and then they let them down. Similar to a hit of caffeine, chemical fertilizers give plants lots of grow power at first and then they crash. Excessive chemical fertilizing weakens plants and eventually causes their susceptibility to pests and diseases. Only compromised plants succumb to blight.

Severe root burn can occur easily from over-fertilizing. Cut the amount in half that they tell you to use on the package. Off the main roots there are tiny tender root hairs through which plants take in water and nutrients. It is easy to burn these hairs with too much fertilizer, particularly if the plant is dry when you dump in the food. To avoid root burn, soak the plant first with plain water and then fertilize.

If you grow plants in a rich potting soil mix that contains organic matter and then add a little bonemeal, your plants shouldn't need much fertilizing. Liquid organic fish emulsion is a good alternate choice to chemical fertilizers. Be sure you dilute it with water according to the directions on the bottle. If you have a fish tank, use the water. You'll be amazed at the boost it gives your plants.

There are many good organic fertilizers on the market now. Use them in the spring and summer, when plants appreciate fertilizers. Plant growth slows down in winter because of lower temperatures and less light. In winter, your tendency might be to pump up your plants, but think about it first. Winter is rest time in the plant kingdom.

Don't expect much new growth in winter. Fertilize less.
Give your plants a break.

Pest Control

If you are giving your plants what they need, balanced
and regular watering, correct light, and a good soil mix, it
is unlikely you will have a pest problem. In a way, plants
are like people. If you maintain them properly, the likeli-
hood of disease lessens. Just as the body heals itself when
given the proper conditions, plants will resist any onslaught of pests or diseases if their needs are being met.

The most common way gardens become infested is
when a new plant is introduced into their midst. For the
sake of your garden, check thoroughly for bugs and diseases before you bring home a new plant. Look on the un-
dersides of leaves, along the stems, in the crotches
between stem and leaves, and inside the tip growth. Pests
love those tender new shoots.

In your home, if you notice bugs or disease, isolate the
plant immediately. Pests can travel from plant to plant,
particularly whitefly. Sometimes you may notice these
teensy white specks fly up from a plant when you touch
the leaves or brush up against them. Otherwise, you may
not even notice whitefly. They sit on the rims of pots or
skim the top of the soil, too. Moisture and mildew, results
of overwatering, are a favorite breeding ground.

Other pests such as mealy bugs, tiny white cottony-
looking things on leaves or in stem crotches, seem to be
drawn to plants that are weakened by overwatering.

Aphids and scale may not be noticeable at first, but their sticky deposit glistens on leaves and stems, and may be your first indication of infestation. Aphids come in different colors. White and green are most common. Scale is brown and crispy. If you catch scale early enough, it will be easier to eradicate simply by wiping with a soapy sponge. You may need to use your fingers to scrape them off, but when they are young, they are easy to remove. The ones on my ficus tree had camped out on its branches for so long, their mature hard shells looked like minuscule turtles. When they are adult, they attach to the leaves and are virtually impossible to remove.

If you are an attentive gardener, you will be checking your plants often to see how they are doing. This care will insure prompt identification of pests or disease. When you do notice something unusual, don't ignore it and hope it will go away. This is wishful thinking. Do something practical as soon as possible. All that may be needed is a good washing with nondetergent soap and warm water. This process is easier and more fun if you can carry the plant to the kitchen sink or bathtub. You will see an immediate relief exude from the plant. The leaves will be brighter, bouncier, and greener.

You can use cotton dipped in alcohol to dab off mealy bugs. Alcohol dessicates the aphids and breaks down their waxy cuticle. In this instance, it's fine to use alcohol. But you know how drying alcohol can be to your skin? Plant leaves react to it in the same way.

Plants that are too lacy or delicate to wipe will need to be sprayed. There are nontoxic home remedies you can make into sprays. In one quart of water, add one to two drops of nondetergent soap and shake. Spray liberally on plants. Whatever home remedy you use, repeat every day for three or four days or until you see results. If nothing looks different after a few days, another remedy may be in order.

Nicotine tea is good to eradicate unwanted bugs in soil. Soak a handful of pipe tobacco in a quart of water. When the tea looks strong, pour it through your plant. It will kill the pests but not the roots. For pests on foliage, cayenne pepper spray often works wonders. You can use fresh hot peppers, too. Blend a half cup of hot peppers with two cups of water and strain liquid for spray. Dilute with extra water, at first, so you can test for potency. Be careful of your skin and eyes. It will burn you, too. Garlic juice and water also works as a spray for bugs and pests, as does straight garlic juice right on the affected areas.

With any of these remedies, repeat the treatment often to be sure the critters don't multiply. Again, the best pest control is attentive care and maintenance of your plants. If a plant is strong and healthy, it will not be hospitable to pests and disease. Keep in mind the ficus tree story. Sometimes plants will surprise you and coexist with critters, and everything turns out all right. So don't be in a hurry to throw away a plant. You never know what can happen if you are part of the negotiations.

On a very direct level, we can broaden our perspective and see plants in relationship to the whole environment in which they live. For example, I know a woman who has a very stunted-looking yard. The plants don't die but they don't grow and flourish either. When I walk on the path to her front door, I get a pained feeling in my heart.

One day she asked me why I thought her bougainvillea wasn't blooming. We walked outside to look at it together and I realized they had a bird feeder staked into the ground right in front of the plant. The birds would alight on the bougainvillea and leave droppings all over it. Covered with white, this ten-year-old vine with thick, strong intertwining stems rested against a lattice neither dying nor growing. This bougainvillea was mature and should have grown up and over the roof of the house, enveloping it with brilliant color.

I told the woman my theory, and at first she couldn't believe it. She wondered why bird poop should keep it from growing. When I asked her how she would feel if she was being dumped on all the time, she laughed and admitted I might have a point. I suggested she move the bird feeder, hose down the leaves, clean them up as best she could and prune back the bougainvillea so it could start fresh. It worked, and she was amazed that the solution was so simple. Then she admitted to me her gardener was a "hacker." He didn't know anything about pruning and just came in and hacked the plants. I told her I could tell by how I felt when I walked through the garden. She began to trust her instincts and see life from the plants' point of view.

Laying the Groundwork

Each region of the United States has different growing conditions and therefore different gardening needs. But, there are general hints that will help you in your garden and complement your inner philosophy. Observe, have patience, and learn to sense when to intervene and when not to. In order to be a sensitive gardener, the more you look, feel, listen, touch, smell, and poke around, the more you will know what is going on. Open yourself so you can feel what is coming to you from the plants. Have patience with them and with yourself. Gardening does not necessarily bestow instant gratification. Besides zeroing in on individual plants, see if you can scan your garden and get an overview. Be both expansive and focused. By having both viewpoints, you will better know when to intervene and when not to. Most of the time, it is best not to. Your garden has a better chance of being balanced if you have a broad spectrum of plants, as in nature, than if you plant a lot of one thing.

Visit other people's gardens. Take walks in your neighborhood. See what other people are doing. Inspiration is available everywhere you look. Windowboxes, postage stamp gardens, borders, front door landscaping, stairways, decks, terraces, and fire escapes are all sources for ideas. Look for opportunities to join community gardens, school gardens, seniors gardens, or start one yourself.

Read the basic information on seed packets and nursery plants. Placement of plants, planting seasons, heights of plants are all factors that cannot be ignored. For example, you shouldn't plant too close together unless you have dug intensive beds in which the soil, rich in organic matter and compost, is loose and friable at least one foot down. Then the roots can run deep. If you are planting conventionally, roots need side room to spread.

Plants need the proper light. Picking the right spot may take time. Spend quiet moments in your garden so you can feel what each place needs. Follow your thoughts and feelings to help you choose the appropriate plant, shrub, flower, or tree. It takes at least two years to feel settled in a garden. When you find yourself rushing, try to slow down.

When moving indoor plants to the outdoors, do it gradually so they can acclimate in stages. Too much light can be harmful to protected indoor plants. Place plants in the shade first and then slowly increase the intensity of light. If you don't do this, the plants will go into shock, even if you tell them what you are doing and why. Cooperation and communication is a give-and-take proposition. You are helping the plants to do what they do naturally. The magic comes in subtle ways. A spiritual approach to gardening doesn't take you away from the earth and the here and now. It brings you closer to who you are, what you are doing, and your relationship with all living things.

The best time to water outdoors is early morning or late afternoon when the sun isn't too intense. Water on leaves in the heat of the day can burn plants and cause discoloration. If you water too late at night, after dark, it can lead to mildew and rot. If your plants have gone limp during the hottest part of the day, don't worry. They will return to normal in the coolness of evening, if you are watering properly. In summer, you may have to water vegetables and flowers more than once a day if there is a heat wave.

Honing your powers of observation will make it easier to detect pests. But the real issue is soil. Plants do not do well in depleted soil. Chemical fertilizers kill those red beneficial earthworms and deaden soil. Food grown in depleted soil will be empty of nutrients and lack flavor and plants will lack vitality. Healthy plants are *green*. Survey your garden. Are the leaves upright and turgid? Are the surfaces glossy or shiny? Do you feel a sense of vibrance coming from the plants? If you don't feel it, it's not there. If you are watering regularly and the plants are receiving the right amount of light, there are no pests or disease, but they are still yellow, then the soil is the problem.

In conventional, nonorganic gardening, the way to get rid of aphids, for example, is to use toxic chemical bug sprays. This kills off their balancer, ladybugs. Aphids multiply faster than ladybugs, so the next infestation will be worse. It's kind of like taking antibiotics. Yes, antibiotics kill harmful bacteria, but they also kill friendly bacteria. The body's friendly flora needs to be replaced. If it is not, the lack of friendly bacteria leads to a greater susceptibility to immune-deficiency diseases and the need for another round or two of antibiotics, which leads to more depletion and the downward spiral continues.

Try natural alternative solutions to toxic chemical sprays and systemic solutions. Often, a simple strong hosing down of a plant with water will remove aphids and discourage their return. Nondetergent soap and water, a few drops per quart of water, can rid a plant of ants in one heavy dosage of spray. Repeat, if necessary. Insecticidal soaps, homemade pepper spray, and garlic spray will work. You do not want to eradicate the helpful bug and earthworm population. Use them as allies. Cooperate with them.

Which brings us back to soil. Healthy, rich soil guarantees healthy plants if water, light, and care are also in balance. Compost and natural organic matter are the key to healthy, alive soil, rich with helpful earthworms and a well-balanced nutrient content. If you are unable to make your own compost, try to find some. Some towns have a community compost system.

Composting happens naturally in nature through partial decay of plant and animal matter. Look underneath the natural mulch of fallen leaves and see the crumbly dark humus that has been produced there. You can stimulate the process by building a compost pile. Combining fruit and vegetable scraps and yard trimmings in a variety of composting systems, will turn them into *humus*, a sweet-smelling crumbly black loam that is both a soil fertilizer and conditioner. It sounds like I'm describing a good shampoo, doesn't it?

A good compost looks almost like coffee grounds, gardeners call brown gold. Turn it into your soil, spread it across the topsoil, use it as a mulch, sprinkle it into your lawn, around plants, under trees, and add it to your houseplants. Compost helps the soil hold water better and you won't have to spend money on fertilizers because you have the best. Your plants will display a new vitality almost immediately.

Food from a composted garden tastes sweet, tender, and delicious. Compost returns minerals to the soil and it is the mineral content that sweetens the food. Once you eat food like this, you will have a hard time returning to store-bought fruits and vegetables that are overbred for good looks but lack in taste. When was the last time you tasted a really sweet and juicy tomato from the store?

Composting can be done in different ways, even indoors, depending on how much effort you want to make. There are rodent resistant bins for outdoors, open piles for yard trimmings only, holes in the ground that need to be dug each time you enter food scraps, manageable worm bins for indoors and outdoors, and closed-air systems for both.

Composting is the philosophical backbone of an inner perspective on gardening and farming. Look at it as a transformational process. Vegetable scraps and plant trimmings are changed back into the substance from whence they came. Garbage becomes sweet smelling and useful once again.

Making compost is like cooking a divine soup. You add together various organic elements that heat up, decompose, and, in a good compost, mutually balance and regulate each other. As you turn the pile or add vegetable scraps, wet leaves, yard trimmings, and grass clippings, you are also adding yourself as an ingredient. As in any creative endeavor, integrating yourself with your creation is a vital part of making good compost. Composting cannot be a strictly mechanical process.

Composting teaches one of the fundamental lessons of gardening. Life is happening, even if you can't see it, everywhere and at all times, even in death. The never-ending process of life, death, and rebirth is enacted right before your eyes. Plants that you consider weeds because they don't fit into the scheme of your garden, vegetable and fruit scraps, green and brown trimmings, can all be utilized in another incarnation in the compost. There is no plainer demonstration of the oneness of all life than the composting of all these disparate elements into one. Everything becomes soil in the end. The earth literally *is* the mother of us all.

TEN

On Other People's Stories: Sowing the Seed

What a wonderful life I've had. I only wish I had realized it sooner.

—Colette

When I speak at workshops and clubs, I learn more and more about the healing power of inner gardening by listening to other people's stories. One way I elicit these stories is through writing exercises. Most people who love to garden are already inner gardeners. Some know it; others don't. By sharing gardening experiences, it is easy to see how we cultivate ourselves when we cultivate a garden. We translate spiritual philosophy into practical work.

Many participants become highly motivated after writing down their ideas. They make connections in their own lives that are instructive and revealing. The process of examining their experience on paper brings self-confidence, clarity, and reflection. They can't wait to go back to their gardens with new awareness. Even nongardeners say the experience inspires them to give gardening a try.

At Sherman Library and Gardens in Corona del Mar, California, I listed one of my workshops as *The Inner Philosophy of Gardening: A Forum to Explore the Healing and Self-Discovery Available Through Communication and Cooperation with the Plant Kingdom*. The group had a very staid appearance, one which belied their emotional connection to the subject. After I spoke about my own experiences with plants and we all traded ideas, I asked people to write for ten minutes on the subject, "Why Do I Garden?" beginning with the phrase, "I garden because . . ." My only other stipulation was that they write continuously, without stopping to edit, organize, or check spelling. I would take care of watching the time.

I scanned their faces while they wrote. One woman started to cry, huddling over her paper to get closer to her thoughts. When the time elapsed, I asked for volunteers to read their work. The woman who cried raised her hand immediately, so I motioned for her to begin. She read a few lines and then broke down completely. She couldn't go on.

The next woman appeared to be in her early sixties. She was stunning, with silvery hair that glinted in the sunlight. She pulled it back into a chignon at the nape of her neck, allowing us a good look at her soft, blue eyes. Simply dressed, her silver jewelry added a quiet elegance to her peaceful demeanor. She was an artistic woman who made an immediate impression with her inner and outer beauty.

She wrote about taking care of her three children during the fifties, nursing them all, even though it wasn't fashionable. In fact, breast-feeding was frowned upon in that era. She had been a very busy new mother since the babies were born so close together. But, whenever the children took their naps, she went out into the garden to work, she loved it so. Inevitably, she said, when she gardened, her milk would begin to flow and she would have to return inside to nurse.

A big sigh went up from the crowd. Everyone marveled at this story of the ultimate symbol of nurturing feminine energy, milk, streaming from a woman's breasts as she played in her garden. Her body obviously was very in tune with her emotional connection to the plants. It was refined enough to turn on the faucet, even when she nurtured the earth.

The next reader was a big woman, with short, curly gray hair. She wore a white blouse with a red velvet bow at the collar and a navy pleated skirt. She looked very businesslike. I was pleasantly surprised when she read her piece. She made herself so vulnerable.

It seems that when she was younger and her children were small, she and her husband took them on a trip to Yosemite. It was mid-afternoon and everyone had gone off to explore. She decided to rest and be quiet so she could replenish.

She sat under a giant redwood tree and breathed a sigh of relief to be alone for a while. Eventually she looked up and saw shafts of light pouring in through the branches of a gargantuan tree. As she sat and watched, fully feeling the moment, she had an epiphany. She said, suddenly she saw the whole world in that tree. She experienced the interconnectedness of all life, and she cried.

As she read, her voice choked up and her face reddened with intense feeling. She told everyone that up until that time in Yosemite, she hadn't understood about gardening with her soul. After that experience, she knew what it meant and it changed her forever.

When the workshop was over, the only man in the audience came up to me. I noticed him throughout. He seemed very withdrawn and had difficulty reading his piece. I thought, perhaps, he was holding back tears.

When we were alone, he told me his daughter was dying of cancer and he was her primary caretaker. He drove her to Mexico for alternative medical treatments and helped her while she went through this very painful process. He started to cry, saying he wished his daughter had the same feeling about plants as we did. His love of gardening recharged and uplifted him. "But," he added, "you can't give that to another person. They have to find it for themselves."

Once, I gave a two-hour call-in interview on a listener-sponsored radio show called "Seeing Beyond" out of Santa Cruz, California. We talked about gardening as a healing experience, for children as well as for adults, whether one gardens indoors or outdoors.

A woman called in, very excited, speaking rapidly with great feeling about an old wisteria vine she had to cut down. It wrapped itself around her porch and invaded the plumbing which caused many problems. She said at the time she cried, overcome with emotion. She didn't understand then why she was crying and felt embarrassed in front of her husband for acting like such a fool. He thought she was nuts. Now she understood the reason for her tears. She was glad to hear other people felt the same way.

Everyone has plant stories. Writing them down clarifies their meaning. Committing your ideas and observations to paper will alter you. You will have to examine what you know and what you think you know. Explore what is true for you. Once you begin, your own story will unfold. The more you welcome it and give it a voice, the more story you will generate.

I have a friend Jana who is a superb landscape architect. She has won many awards for her wild gardens. At Christmas she made her own greeting card using Japanese calligraphy to illustrate her impressions of the plant world. Accompanying this drawing on earthy brown paper stock was a short message about her experience with the rose fairy in a New York subway. She made an unemotional and intelligent plea to inspire all the recipients of her cards "to pay attention to the fairies wherever they are and give them your support because without them, not only our gardens but the entire world would be a very sad place." She mailed out hundreds of these cards to friends, relatives, and clients. I was so impressed at her courage to say such a thing to the world. She told me she was surprised how touched everyone was who read it. She received calls from university professors, doctors, lawyers, dentists, and their assistants thanking her for her thoughts. Many of them passed on the card to others, they were so taken with the message. It struck me how times are changing if so many people can relate to mythical beings who remain a mystery but speak to the primitive and the innocent within all of us.

These are the kinds of stories garden club members can share at meetings; docents at botanical gardens can add to their tours; and parents and teachers can include in their science projects with kids. There are more of us than we realize, so have courage. It's time to speak out!

Dear Reader:

I am always interested in experiences and new information about the plant world—please address correspondence to:

Judith Handelsman
P.O. Box 599
Laguna Beach, CA 92652
E-mail address—growmail @aol.com

If you write by hand, please make sure it's legible. Thank you.

Bibliography

Bradley, Fern Marshall, and Barbara W. Ellis, eds. *Rodale's All-New Encyclopedia of Organic Gardening*. Emmaus, PA: Rodale Press, 1992.

Findhorn Community. *The Findhorn Garden*, New York: Harper & Row, 1975.

Goethe, Johann Wolfgang von, *The Metamorphosis of Plants*. Kimberton, PA: Biodynamic Farming and Gardening Association, 1993.

Jeavons, John. *How to Grow More Vegetables Than You Ever Thought Possible on Less Land Than You Can Imagine*. Berkeley, CA: Ten Speed Press, 1974, 1979, 1982.

Kaminski, Patricia, and Richard Katz. *Flower Essence Repertory*. Nevada City, CA: Flower Essence Society, 1986, 1987, 1992, 1994.

Steiner, Rudolf. *Agriculture*. Kimberton, PA: Biodynamic Farming and Gardening Association, 1993.

Storl, Wolf D. *Culture and Horticulture: A Philosophy of Gardening*. Kimberton, PA: Biodynamic Farming and Gardening Association, 1979.

Stout, Ruth, and Richard Clemence. *The Ruth Stout No-Work Garden Book*. Emmaus, PA: Rodale Press, 1971.

Tompkins, Peter, and Christopher Bird. *The Secret Life of Plants*. New York: Harper & Row, 1973.

Tompkins, Peter, and Christopher Bird. *The Secrets of the Soil*. New York: Harper & Row, 1989.

Wildfeuer, Sherry, ed. *Stella Natura* 1993 and *Stella Natura* 1996. Kimberton, PA: Biodynamic Farming and Gardening Association.

Acknowledgments

There are many people I would like to thank for helping me along the way. Carole DeSanti, my editor, gave invaluable direction that changed me and my writing and was consistently kind and compassionate. Connie Clausen, my beloved agent, shared the vision. Without her humor, clarity, and straight talk, this book would never have been as much fun to write. My late father, Sam Handelsman, imparted to me his love of words and enriched my life with his intellect. Although he claimed he was an atheist, he passed on a pantheism of sorts, extending to me his wonder at the mysteries of "Mother Nature." Larry Blue helped me from the very beginning in countless ways. It is to him I owe a debt of gratitude for insisting in 1987 that I "join the twentieth century and learn the computer." Wade Roberts at Sherman Library and Gardens befriended me and backed me, lending his encouragement and time. For all he has given, I am grateful. I admire my dear friend Jana Ruzicka, for her kindred spirit, her unbridled creativity and clear-sighted articulation of those things ineffable. Z'ev Rosenberg helped me come back to life. Jacqueline Welles inspired me and made me laugh. Mimi Nelson has been a second mother. Rochelle Reed-Smith helped shape my focus in the early stages, graciously giving me the benefit of her sophisticated overview and highly developed expertise. Maury Solomon read my first attempts, shared her opinions, and gave encouragement. I appreciate my friend Craig Fisher for his company, great conversation, and goodness and Bob Nero, for being the Buddha in the Venice garden. Charline Grogan was very generous with herself. Linda Blinn recognized a flower fairy. Gep Durenberger, at the Decorative Arts Study Center, appreciated the manuscript in its incipient stages and urged me to continue. For his warmth and compassionate nature, I salute him. Linda Weidlinger at the library of the C. G. Jung Institute of Los Angeles offered enthusiastic assistance. I honor Jennifer Hagl, a beloved friend and an imaginative gardener, for the sensitive and artistic way she does everything. Eileen King shared her clarity and understanding of Anthroposophy in a very personal, articulate, and loving way. I thank Sherry Wildfeuer, editor of the *Stella Natura*, the Kimberton Hills Agricultural Calendar, a publication of the Biodynamic Farming and Gardening Association. Sherry's writing illuminated Anthroposophy and Biodynamics for me. Linda Binley made astute and thought-provoking suggestions. Deborah Rogers gave moral support. Karen Klein offered a fresh eye. Greg Smith found my favorite poem when I thought all was lost. Most of all, I thank the plant kingdom for giving me this book to write.